PRAISE FOR
# The Magic of Yes

"*The Magic of Yes* by Lori Pappas is a transformative guide that empowers women to embrace their potential and pursue their dreams with confidence. Through relatable stories and insightful lessons, Pappas illustrates how to break free from limiting beliefs and cultivate a life aligned with your true self. This book is not just a road map; it's a call to action for every woman seeking inspiration and validation. With practical advice and heartfelt wisdom, Pappas encourages us to say yes to our curiosity and strength, reminding us that the journey to self-discovery is both essential and rewarding. Dive into these pages and unlock the magic within you!"

—Amelia M. Duran-Stanton, PhD, DSc, MPAS, author of *The LOTUS Within: Grow Your Purpose and Ignite Your Passion*

"This powerful book reveals how saying yes to challenge and change can catalyze extraordinary personal growth. Drawing from her remarkable journey, Pappas provides a practical road map for transformation that will resonate with anyone who has ever faced failure and wondered, *What next?*"

—Joe Sipher, author of *Outsmart the Learning Curve*, entrepreneur, product and marketing executive, mentor

"In *The Magic of Yes: Embrace the Wise Woman Within*, author Lori Pappas offers sound and time-tested working premises for the expected and unexpected curveballs that life may throw our way. As a longtime practitioner in the field of leadership, team building, and organization development, I have seen these principles at work in many settings. The key to their success is scrupulous application; we must play our part. Make the necessary effort, and the universe will smile on us! *The Magic of Yes* offers excellent navigation guidelines, and although it addresses women directly, these principles apply to men too. Highly recommended."

—Michael Shandler, EdD, award-winning author of the memoir *Karma & Kismet: A Spiritual Quest Across Continents, Cultures, and Consciousness*

"*The Magic of Yes* is an uplifting book for anyone who wants to be deeply inspired and encouraged to live their best life. The author shares openly about her own difficult journey, which is inspiring beyond words. Other touching stories from 'wise women' who have overcome adversity are woven seamlessly into the book, providing valuable lessons and insight. Lori encourages all women to become their authentic selves through living intentionally and saying yes to the things that bring joy and growth into life."

—Helene Zupanc, licensed professional counselor and author of *Sticky Note Mantras: The Art and Science of Choosing Your Thoughts*

"A must-read, Lori Pappas's brilliant book *The Magic of Yes* brings value and relevance to every woman's inherent wisdom. It explores how our inner muse can motivate us to overcome our fears as we reveal our deepest desires and truth."

—Joan E Childs, psychotherapist, inspirational speaker, author of *Do You Hate the One You Love? (Strategies to Heal and Save Your Relationship)*, *Why Did She Jump? (My Daughter's Battle with Bipolar Disorder)*, and *The Myth of the Maiden (On Being a Woman)*

"After reading *The Magic of Yes*, I felt more empowered, motivated, and inspired than ever before. Part memoir, part historical documentary, [the book] helped me peel away my self-doubt, stop 'shoulding' on myself, and access my inner sage. [Pappas's] personal journey is quite a triumph over adversity and speaks to all generations of women."

—Cathy Carroll, president, Legacy Onward, Inc., author of *Hug of War: How to Lead a Family Business with Both Love and Logic*

"*The Magic of Yes* blends encouragement for healing with stories of women overcoming challenges and often wrenching circumstances. . . . In the confident tone of someone who has overcome significant hurdles and challenges, Pappas shares her mission of developing a sense of self-awareness and integrity, distinguishing between one's personal and professional self, and making oneself a top priority with the power of WIIFM (what's in it for me?). . . .

"After becoming a successful businesswoman, Pappas worked in Ethiopia distributing medicine. Some of her stories about the inexcusable abuse that African women faced are difficult to read, but their courage to better their lives is captivating. The numerous stories of women overcoming abuse and adversity offer compassionate advice, reminding readers that they are not alone in their individual experiences—and serving as heartening reminders that cycles of abuse can be broken. Pappas provides contemplative wisdom, grounded advice, and practical lessons for women of all backgrounds who desire self-determination."

—Booklife

"... The author demonstrates the importance of cross-cultural learning, empathy, and getting out of one's comfort zone with examples from her time in Ethiopia's South Omo Valley working with Indigenous communities. . . . Pappas concludes with a wise-woman mantra that calls upon open-mindedness, connection, compassion, and curiosity to foster personal growth and collective well-being. The author's DREAM (Desire, Reflect, Explore, Acknowledge, and Mantra) model (referenced at the end of each chapter) provides a unique structured framework for transformation that readers can use to apply the lessons to their lives. . . . A trauma survivor's deeply personal guide to awakening inner wisdom."

—*Kirkus Reviews*

## Awards:

American Writing Awards: Women's Issues

Mind and Spirit Book Awards
for Non-Fiction Guides and Workbooks

*The Magic of Yes:*
*Embrace the Wise Woman Within*
by Lori Pappas

© Copyright 2025 Lori Pappas

ISBN 979-8-88824-622-1

All rights reserved. No part of this publication may be reproduced, stored in a retrieval system, or transmitted in any form or by any means—electronic, mechanical, photocopy, recording, or any other—except for brief quotations in printed reviews, without the prior written permission of the author.

Published by

**köehlerbooks**™

3705 Shore Drive
Virginia Beach, VA 23455
800-435-4811
www.koehlerbooks.com

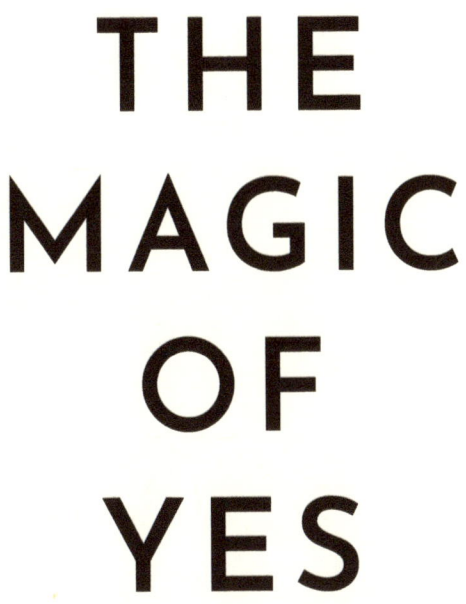

# THE MAGIC OF YES

## Embrace the Wise Woman Within

### LORI PAPPAS

VIRGINIA BEACH
CAPE CHARLES

To Melissa, Shay, David, Ella, James, and Xavia;
the Star Girls of the Hamar tribe, Gulu Bola and Dobe Oita;
and all of you extraordinary ordinary women.

# Table of Contents

Introduction ............................................................. 1
**Part One: Discover Your Essence** .................................. 3
   Chapter 1: Winning with the Cards You've Been Dealt ........ 5
   Chapter 2: Saying No and Setting Boundaries ................ 19
   Chapter 3: Forgiving Yourself and Others ................... 30
   Chapter 4: Being the Curious Entrepreneur
   of Your Own Life ........................................... 44
**Part Two: Navigate Your Chaos** .................................... 59
   Chapter 5: Challenging the Status Quo ...................... 61
   Chapter 6: Understanding the Power of WIIFM ................ 73
   Chapter 7: Taking Risks to Embrace New Opportunities ....... 91
   Chapter 8: Asking for Help 106
**Part Three: Set Yourself Free** ................................... 123
   Chapter 9: Learning from "Different" People and Cultures .. 124
   Chapter 10: Defining Your Own "Supposed-Tos" .............. 138
   Chapter 11: Activating Empathy and Compassion ............. 157
   Chapter 12: Helping Others Help Themselves ................ 172
**Part Four: Find Your Peace** ...................................... 188
   Chapter 13: Stepping Out of Your Comfort Zone ............. 190
   Chapter 14: Embracing Love (and Life) ..................... 204
   Chapter 15: Weeding Your Physiological Garden ............. 219
   Chapter 16: Recognizing the Wise Woman Within ............. 231
Epilogue ............................................................ 245
Acknowledgments ..................................................... 247

# Introduction

People often equate wisdom with age or a wealth of experiences. Not true! There is a chasm of difference between wisdom and experience, and you don't have to be old to be wise. Miles on your body, entry stamps on your passport, and wrinkles on your face don't guarantee wisdom. They just show you were lucky enough to travel and grow old. True wisdom, according to researchers and renowned thinkers, comes from saying "yes" to insatiable curiosity, reflecting deeply on your experiences, extracting lessons, and using those insights to guide your thoughts and actions.

Each of us has the ability to access and embrace our wise woman within. This lifelong personal journey requires continuous learning, taking risks, aligning your actions with your values, and cultivating an attitude of gratitude. Fortunately, you need not travel alone. Stories from my journey, supported with snippets from the lives of extraordinary ordinary women (some names have been changed for privacy), will inspire and give you courage. Research and advice garnered from experts help untangle the complexities and provide steps for growth and mantras to soothe your soul during your quest.

You are surrounded by a sisterhood of wise women, those who have walked this earth before us and many who are here with us today, maybe even living next door. We are available to lend a hand when you stumble, warts and imperfections exposed.

Discover "the magic of yes" by embracing your inner wise woman. Each chapter concludes with suggested DREAM (which stands for desire, reflect, explore, acknowledge, mantra) activities to help you experience greater happiness and more moments of delight and come to feel at peace within your own skin. Your sisters (including me) are cheering for you every step of the way.

# PART ONE

## Discover Your Essence

When you look at yourself in the mirror, the image you see may not reflect the real you! It may be a collage of what you are "supposed" to look like according to your socioeconomic status, education, and family role. The essence of you—your core—demands a deep sense of self-awareness and integrity. It is different from your perceived identity.

I felt like two different people for years. Untangling my identity from my core essence was complicated. I behaved and even processed information differently in my personal life than I did professionally, praised for competency in business but quick to duck into my foxhole at home. The path to merge my personal and professional self was fraught with potholes and unnecessary detours. After decades of making mistakes and finding the courage to pick myself back up again, I am now able to see the *real* me when I look in the mirror—most of the time.

This section, "Discover Your Essence," provides building blocks that promote self-awareness. It suggests examining the traits and factors within your control that can be leveraged, changed, or replaced. When you become adept at saying no and setting boundaries, you are able to protect your mental and physical well-being. When you forgive yourself and others, you no longer carry excess baggage and your personal power increases. This helps you channel your strength and courage to become who you want to be.

# 1

# Winning with the Cards You've Been Dealt

We do not control who we are at birth or the zip code of our arrival. We enter the world with certain genes, innate traits, and built-in potential and with no choice about our family or its social environment, economic status, and religious dynamics. Some of us live in underdeveloped countries, while others reside in rich locales with well-developed infrastructures.

Location, location, location. It determines our biggest "supposed-tos," from spiritual beliefs to civil rights to educational and financial opportunities.

The cards from the original hand we were each dealt may determine how we are perceived: through gender identity, race, being beautiful and bright or ugly and dim, entitled or challenged, aware or oblivious of our surroundings. Some hands come from a mature and nurturing deck, while others are dealt by absent parents or tattered, worn-out souls.

First, congratulations! You made it. You survived your childhood by navigating the challenges and hurdles you encountered along the way, and you did what was necessary to get where you are today. You are a survivor. And best of all, you have an inquisitive spirit and the willingness to grow. Pause for a moment . . . and celebrate you.

We might have arrived in this world with a lucky hand or a lousy deal from a deck we didn't choose or even shuffle, but it's not the only one we get to play. No matter how our place in the world is initially determined or what additional cards we gamble on or receive, each of us will inevitably get a chance to play our own hand. If we want to be the ultimate architects of our lives, we must choose when to draw a new card, such as changing our go-to behaviors (Hello, Miss Impatience or Ms. Numb), and when to discard, such as leaving a toxic relationship (Goodbye, Mr. Abuse-Me-No-More). Self-determination is the key to either improving one's hand or waving the white flag and becoming a victim. Each of us *can* choose our own path, and the process of that journey begins as soon as we have the cognitive ability to make our own independent choices.

As the renowned philosopher Voltaire once said, "Each player must accept the cards life deals him or her, but once they are in hand, he or she must alone decide how to play the cards in order to win the game."

This truth was exemplified by Helen Keller (and her brilliant teacher, Anne Sullivan), both icons of what I call the Wise Women Sisterhood. Ms. Keller was struck blind and deaf at only nineteen months old. Rather than letting her profound disabilities cripple and prevent her from reaching her potential, she converted her weaknesses into strengths. As an educator, organizer, and fundraiser, she was responsible for many advances in public services to the handicapped. Both Sullivan and Keller were self-aware and determined, and each discovered and maximized her authentic self.

As we juggle the chaotic demands of school, career, children, partners, or aging parents, we often lose the connection to the wise woman inside us. Even if we live the "American Dream," we may still feel empty and unfulfilled, and our warrior spirit can be left to wander aimlessly, trying to find its purpose.

## HOLD, FOLD, OR RUN

The road ahead is fraught with potholes and detours, and it takes practice and perseverance to make good choices. Ideally, we make lots of little mistakes quickly, which keeps us from making big ones. Naturally, no one makes good decisions all the time. None of us start out as card sharks. We mess up, hold on to the wrong cards, and discard those that could help us find our personal jackpot.

I started life with a mixed deck. Despite the advantages of innate intelligence, average looks, determination, sufficient healthy food, good education, and shelter, I also suffered profound psychological abuse and post-traumatic stress disorder (PTSD), which required decades of work.

My cards were dealt by two worn and tattered parents: a religious fanatic mother who believed I sinned every time I opened my mouth and a father who committed me to an asylum, hoping I'd learn a new vocabulary. Despite all my parents did, I had to accept responsibility for myself. I needed to find my safe harbor and learn to appreciate my genuine essence.

My starting point was Mahnomen, a poor community in the northwest corner of Minnesota. Our middle-class family appeared to be rich, with a white clapboard house and a swing set in the backyard. Perfect on the outside. Not so much on the inside. While Daddy was a hunter and fisherman and the superintendent of schools, Mother was a card-playing addict who transformed into a religious addict when I was two years old. She became a master of psychological abuse, and I was her target.

The earliest memory I have of my mother was her murmuring, "I love you, Jesus," every minute of every hour of every day. She talked to Jesus much more than she talked to me or my three older sisters. She was God's mouthpiece. She possessed the ultimate "get out of jail free" card: No matter what, she was doing God's will. Over more than fifty years, I don't recall her ever taking responsibility for any of her words or actions.

Mother believed castor oil and enemas cured every earthly ill. From ages three to five, I ran and hid under the table, under my bed, or in the woods whenever I saw her coming. Survival depended on being quick. Mother couldn't run after me because she had a "bad" heart. My sisters and I did all the housework because Mother might have a heart attack at any moment. She never did. A stroke killed her at eighty-six, with a perfectly healthy heart.

Each night, I was forced to pray for forgiveness before I fell asleep because I was a sinner. Jesus might fetch us in the middle of the night, and if I had one speck of sin in me, I would be left behind while the rest of my family was swept up to heaven during the Second Coming. Confused, I questioned how this could be true since babies in Africa didn't know about Jesus, which was so unfair.

*Shame on you! Questioning is a sin. Don't blaspheme. On your knees and pray.*

## WAKE THE WARRIOR

I taught myself to read and swim when I was three. Story characters became my friends. Reading offered a fantasy world of excitement and adventure while swimming competitively gave me a visceral sense of accomplishment. I started piano when I was six. When I was nine, we moved to Robbinsdale, a suburb of Minneapolis, where I studied with former Russian concert pianist Mrs. Smirnow. She taught me to play big, bold classical pieces and express my feelings. I loved to play and practiced for hours. These three outlets—reading, swimming, playing music—worked well until puberty kicked in and my warrior spirit began to flex her muscles!

I desperately wanted to belong, have a peer group, and be accepted. I wanted a voice in determining where I was going and who was going with me. I threw down the gauntlet, and a noisy, messy, chaotic war ensued. Over the next six years, I lost most of the battles.

The innovative local school board formed an accelerated seventh-grade class that would eventually ace their college exams. I was the brightest of the eggheads, but I yearned to be a cool hippie kid. Think *Happy Days*, the Beatles, Mary Ann Faithful, and Joan Baez. Being smart and getting straight As was not cool. I lied about my report card and wore black knee socks with penny loafers, culottes, and men's shirts with a loop in the back whenever I could sneak out of the house, dressed for the in-crowd.

Being an egghead was another part of my mixed deck. I was smart but impatient with people who made decisions slower than I did. I'm still trying to rid myself of that sticky card—which must be glued to my fingers, because impatience haunts me.

I became a championship swimmer at thirteen, and when the popular girls on the team harassed me, I quit. Soon after, my mother decided that I needed to play hymns instead of classical music. She was upset that she couldn't show me off playing Christmas carols. She enrolled me in a religious music school, which I hated, so I refused to practice.

More tension. More resentment. More anger. More blame.

The first major battle of the six-year war occurred that summer. Dad's sister was coming, so Mother told me to clean the cupboards. She wanted Alice to think she was a good housekeeper.

"If you want to be a good housekeeper, clean the cupboard yourself!"

Whoops! Buttons pushed, Mother followed me into the bathroom and locked the door. Startled, I spun around and shrieked at her, "Get out of here! Leave me alone."

She blocked the door, trapping me inside. Her face flushed, chest heaving, she shook her finger an inch from my face.

"I command you to get out of my daughter. What is your name?"

I laughed nervously. "Duh. Lori. You named me, remember?"

"No! That's not your name. You are the devil! You are not my daughter."

My friend was in my bedroom, and, embarrassed and mortified, I worried she would hear my deranged mother.

"What is your name? Get out of my daughter. Satan, I command you!"

I shoved her aside as I escaped the house with my friend.

Later, my mother took me to her favorite pastor. They decided that by combining their energy, they could force the devil out of me. They sat me in a chair, and the onslaught began.

"Satan, what is your name? I command you to get out! What is your name?"

Again and again and again. Knee to knee. In my face.

They didn't get the devil's name that day. I left that room of horrors still named Lori, but something shifted. Whenever I felt anxious, I hyperventilated, disassociated, and hovered over my body as an observer, watching every movement and twitch of my face before losing consciousness and crumpling to the ground. This was devastating when it happened in a hallway at school—miles away from "cool."

## THE DEVIL MADE ME DO IT

The "You are the devil" period of my life is an extreme example of psychological abuse. According to the National Coalition Against Domestic Violence, psychological abuse has been experienced by approximately 50 percent of adults.[1] Common behaviors include humiliation, controlling what the victim can or cannot do, demeaning the victim in public or in private, and refusing access to money or activities.

Psychological abuse increases the trauma of physical and sexual abuse. Several studies demonstrate that it causes long-term damage to a

---

1 "Domestic Violence Statistics," National Domestic Violence Hotline, accessed September 23, 2024, https://www.thehotline.org/stakeholders/domestic-violence-statistics/.

victim's mental health, including depression, PTSD, suicidal ideation, low self-esteem, and difficulty trusting others. Subtle psychological abuse can be more harmful than overt psychological abuse or direct aggression.

Forty years passed before I learned that the trauma caused by my mother's attempt to cure my rebellious nature triggered PTSD. Although I shrugged it off at the time, this period was so stressful and frightening that it influenced my behavior for decades.

My automatic physiological response of fleeing from perceived threats or danger changed. As a child, I had to physically run away from castor oil and enemas. By the time I was a teenager, I hyperventilated and lost consciousness whenever I was overwhelmed by anxiety.

I won a few small battles, like sneaking out of the house every Saturday night until my mother checked my bedroom and locked my window. How dare she? I rang the doorbell repeatedly until she answered and fled early the next morning before my dad got up. Luckily, one of my sisters lived nearby, and when Dad showed up at her door, she saved me from a beating by denying I was there. When he cooled off, I went home and prepared for the next battle.

The rules of engagement changed when I was the only kid left at home. My oldest sister, Kathy, the pleaser, was married to a very religious guy. She would hide me, but her husband wouldn't lie. Willow, the scapegoat, was married and living in Seattle, and Eileen, the manipulator, was attending college in California.

All eyes focused on me, and Mother did not like what she saw—an older, taller version of the devil's child, too tough and clever to bully. Time to move me out. Mother convinced Dad that Augustana Academy, a strict boarding school in South Dakota, was the answer. I could skip eleventh grade and become an instant senior, under the thumb of religious zealots.

I hyperventilated during chapel one day and ended that venture. I was shipped back home immediately and quickly subjected to Mother's next experiment: barbiturates. She convinced our family doctor that I needed pills to make me compliant. She failed to tell my dad.

One evening, he saw Mother give me a handful of pills, flew into a rage, and pinned her against the wall, hands around the neck, choking her. Mother called out to Jesus to save her, and Dad squeezed tighter. I managed to pry them apart and coerce him downstairs. He sat in my green rocking chair and kept chanting how much he hated her. I perked right up. Now was my chance! I tried to convince him to divorce her. I confided that I had prayed for them to split up since I was a little girl; I wanted to live with only him.

But that didn't work. Nope. Dad's rigid view of right versus wrong did not tolerate divorce. Years later, during our last lunch together before he died, he lamented that he was a failure as a dad—not because he ignored my mother's psychological abuse but because I had just filed to divorce my first husband.

When I realized that Dad would never leave my mother, I became depressed. I had just finished reading *I Never Promised You a Rose Garden* and was curious if slitting my wrists would really kill me. I decided to give it a try, but I barely went deep enough to bleed. Next experiment was to try hanging myself with a curtain cord while lying in bed. Can't remember how I came up with that dumb idea. Obviously I wasn't serious, but I made a huge mistake in telling the truth when my parents asked why I had a Band-Aid on my wrist.

A few days later, they hustled me off to a psychiatrist. After the doctor talked to me and my parents separately, he said he believed me and wanted to admit my mother into a hospital to deal with her abusive behavior. Dad refused to go along because everyone would know that he had married damaged goods. Instead, my father chose to have me admitted to Glenwood Hills Mental Hospital "to teach me how to live with my mother" because that was the only way to end the battles in our house. I was a minor. I had no voice.

Next thing I knew, I was stumbling down an antiseptic-smelling hallway, dizzy, filled with experimental psychotic drugs, careening off the walls.

*Head down. Don't look. Be invisible.*

Dad left me at the nuthouse perched on a hillside in beautiful Golden Valley. Soon, I had no idea how long I'd been there. I could barely shuffle one foot ahead of the other. My mind was fuzzy, like scratchy steel wool. My stomach ached. I was confused and disoriented. They gave me little paper cups filled with strange-looking pills. "Just take a sip of water and swallow them down, dear."

I was scared. At one point, when my feet felt heavy, my legs tingled, and I could barely move, I hyperventilated. Blackout!

When I woke up, two girls were sitting on my bed. Little Donna was moaning.

"Tomorrow, they are going to shock me again. I begged them 'No more,' but they won't listen. They said if I refuse, they're going to do a lobotomy. I'm scared. What should I do?"

Her sobs grew louder. Jane patted Donna's back and shook her head. I wondered, *What the heck is going on?* I slowly connected the dots to figure out why I felt so muddled. *The pills.* The nurse came again with her little paper cups. *Do not swallow the pills.* I hid them in my cheek, took a sip of water, swallowed, and when the nurse left, I spit them into a Kleenex and hid them in my pocket. My head throbbed, and I tried to sleep.

The next day, Dr. Barry, the psychiatrist who admitted me, entered my room for his "fix Lori" session. I put my plan in action. I listened to his questions carefully so I could answer them just right. I had to figure out what he wanted to hear. (My first "What's in it for me?"/ WIIFM moment. See chapter 7.) I knew I needed to behave a certain way to get out of there. Maybe Jane, the older girl, could tell me what to do. I asked to be reassigned to her room.

Operation "Get Outta Here" was underway.

It took me a month to convince Dr. Barry I was not suicidal. I told him I was excited to go to a Lutheran college near Seattle, which my dad and I had reluctantly agreed on. I promised I would never again live in the same house as my mother. The day after I was discharged, I boarded a train and traveled three days across the country by myself.

I had just "celebrated" my seventeenth birthday alone in the hospital.

The first time I tried to read after leaving the asylum, I discovered that my photographic memory had disappeared. I read a page of *For Whom the Bell Tolls* by Ernest Hemingway, closed my eyes, and tried to recall what I had just read. I failed, so I read the page again. Same. Read it again. Same. Fifty years later, I still have problems. My long-term memory is good, but my short-term can be iffy.

My emotional escape mechanism of hyperventilating was replaced with hypervigilance and a feeling of being "on edge" (hyperarousal). My emotions were numbed, but my antenna was on high alert. PTSD caused me to withdraw into myself whenever I sensed danger. I formed a protective body armor to deflect arrows from possible attack. This behavior stunted my personal growth.

## ANYTHING BUT A LOVE CHILD

I worked in a dive café in Seattle until the Pacific Lutheran University term started. Things went smoothly until the day Mother picked up the extension when I made a routine call to my father. When I told her to hang up, my dad came unglued. He wrote me a letter saying that Mother was right; I *was* possessed by the devil. My fragile world shattered into a million pieces.

I packed my bags, grabbed my cheap guitar, and fled to Canada. When the bus stopped at the border, the guard discovered I was underage and returned me to Seattle. Next plan: Fly to Alaska. But I didn't have enough money to take my guitar. Sitting in the bus station, I felt desperate. I figured the college had notified my father that I was missing. I had to go somewhere fast if I wanted my freedom, so I purchased a ticket to San Francisco with my few remaining dollars.

As I got off the bus, an internal voice whispered in my ear, *Call Dad.* Good thing I did because I had been reported missing. But I lucked out. It was Election Day, and missing teenagers were a low priority.

Dad apologized profusely for his letter. He understood why I was devastated and instructed me to get a room at the YWCA. As soon as the receptionist checked my ID, she called the police to report me as a runaway. Since my dad knew where I was, I wasn't arrested, but being underage meant I couldn't rent a room at the Y.

I was dealt an ace when a woman in the lobby who was waiting for the receptionist to get off work overheard my story and said I could come live with her—no questions asked. It was 1966. Interesting times.

I paid $15 a week for a room with a shared toilet down the hall. My guardian angel, Marie, had recently retired from JCPenney and helped me get a job wrapping packages. It was Thanksgiving, and I was living by myself near Haight Ashbury during the height of the free-love era. Fortunately for me, I was terrified of drugs.

One lonely night, a moment of clarity hit: *I need to be responsible for myself. No matter what my parents did, I am the only one who can change the trajectory of my life. I must create the building blocks of who I want to become. It's on me. I am the only one who can do this for myself.*

### Dancing with Discomfort

Katheryn Trenshaw certainly wasn't born in the most advantageous location. The ghetto in Gary, Indiana, where she was raised in the 1960s was so volatile that her older brother was shot dead at thirteen while playing one evening. And her health (as a two-time stage 3 cancer survivor) definitely left something to be desired. But Katheryn is smart, resilient, and an amazing creative, determined to keep her challenges from defining her life.

Katheryn's work as a radical well-being facilitator has always been about embracing and finding comfort in discomfort and focusing her creative energy on helping people from all walks of life find freedom in authenticity. In 2012, she started the In Your Own Skin project. She poured her life savings into traveling around the world, asking people the unflinching question "What is true of you but not obvious to strangers?" and then writing it on their skin and filming their interviews and snippets of their lives. This became her innovative, provocative *In Your Own Skin* documentary and book. *In Your Own Skin* reveals what is concealed in people, ranging from urban street dancers in New York City to an international rock star.

Katheryn invites us to inquire, "What is most essential? We are not going to live forever. What meaningful, authentic way of being have you engaged in today?"

### LETTING GO TO WIN

For more than thirty years, I had violent nightmares. In each one, I was killed or maimed. I was finally able to process the events and move on from these traumas during my stint at the Sierra Tucson rehab center in 2005. Once the memories were processed, the nightmares disappeared. I still shut down, however, when someone raises their voice at me.

Being a victim and having a victim mentality are different. Being a victim is temporary and generally outside of our control. Victimhood, or having a victim mentality, is using the condition of having been hurt, damaged, or made to suffer to make people feel sorry for us or as an excuse for our behavior. The opposite of victimhood is accountability. While our circumstances may not be our fault, they are our responsibility. How we respond to our circumstances can change the outcome.

We now know that PTSD causes changes in the brain. Studies show that parts of the brain involved in emotional processing appear different in scans of people with PTSD; the structure responsible for memory and emotions, known as the hippocampus, is smaller.

Scientists think the malfunctioning hippocampus may prevent flashbacks and nightmares from being properly processed. When the anxiety generated does not reduce over time, it can result in increased fear, anxiety, and memory problems.

Not all of my original circumstances were terrible: My mother had proper nutrition when she was pregnant, so I was born with healthy cognitive skills. I had enough food to eat, shelter, and clothing. I am intelligent, curious, and determined. However, the residue of the bad parts stayed with me for more than fifty years. I developed a toolkit of unhealthy coping skills, which included numbing out, working constantly, and running away from personal conflict.

I have learned a lot since those days. It's become clear that winning with the cards you were dealt has less to do with your opening hand than the hand you end up with and how you play it. That's what ultimately matters.

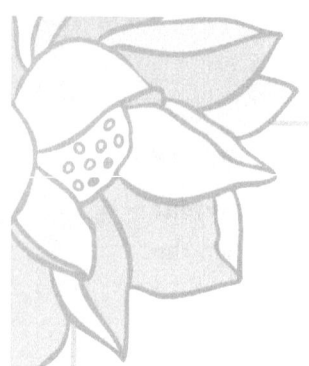

# DREAM:
## *Winning with the Cards I've Been Dealt*

**D**esire: Be the best possible version of me.

**R**eflect on my strengths and identify which ones can be leveraged for good.

**E**xplore how I can use my experiences to create a better present and future for myself and others.

**A**cknowledge that I have special talents available to use to reach my fullest potential.

**M**antra:
Stand by me, hold my hand,
Open my eyes, that I may clearly see the goodness in me.

### WISE WOMAN WORDS

"Owning our story can be hard
but not nearly as difficult as
spending our lives running from it."
--Brené Brown, *The Gifts of Imperfection*

# 2

# Saying No and Setting Boundaries

"Be good and do what you are told," says Mother, Father, teacher, and every other authority figure in our lives when we are little. "Being good" means acquiescing, accommodating, and being agreeable. We are programmed to comply in order to make others feel good, promote harmony, and keep the peace. Praised for saying yes and spanked for saying no. *Do you recall ever hearing a child praised for saying no or rebelling?*

The act of saying no and setting boundaries feels foreign and uncomfortable to most of us. We were trained to please, not to disappoint. Compliance may not have been rewarded, but defiance was punished. Many of us grew up thinking being abused was normal. The pressure to be good may have caused us to experience victimhood.

To move past victimization requires conscious choice, hard work, and overcoming the guilty feeling of not being compliant. It can be scary and painful to travel this pathway. We need courage to keep picking ourselves up when we stumble and fall. There is a difference between being good and being a good person (one who is kind, compassionate, empathetic, and acts with integrity). As self-awareness increases, we start facing the fears that force us to be compliant. With greater self-confidence, we gain the courage to overcome the fear of rejection and/or abandonment, fear of upsetting someone, and fear of being alone.

Conversely, if our response to being victimized is to develop a victim's mindset, we stay stuck in the past, and our ability to grow is stunted. It is even more difficult if we are involved in a codependent relationship or friendship, where the "giver" (us) does everything in their power to keep the other person happy, while the "taker" contributes little to nothing to make the giver happy.

To grow and flourish, we need to accept that setting boundaries is a healthy and necessary part of maintaining balanced relationships and personal well-being.

Setting professional boundaries wasn't difficult for me, but setting personal boundaries has been a lifetime challenge. Yes, I was a rebellious child. My warrior spirit was alive and kicking, although she wasn't very effective. I was still a personal mess when I was released from the nuthouse. I had the courage to rebel—but not the confidence nor self-worth to set healthy boundaries to protect myself.

## GROWING UP WITH CONFUSING BOUNDARIES

Our house was full of conflicting messages. Mother certainly did not respect the physical bodies of her daughters, especially when she was armed with her bottle of castor oil and the enema bag. We were also not allowed to deviate from her version of Christianity. Intellectual curiosity was encouraged only if it was confined to *Encyclopedia Britannica*. No talking back, no disagreement, acquiesce, be good.

We moved from Mahnomen, Minnesota, to Lewistown, Montana, when I was four years old. Lewistown is in the exact center of Montana, and in the 1950s it had a population of 6,500. Dad was the school superintendent. We lived in a two-story corner house on Corcoran Avenue that had a screen door my sisters loved to slam in my face. Mother became addicted to juicing vegetables, and her specialty was bean sprouts. Kathy and Willow refused to drink her concoctions, but I had no voice and no choice. My only defense was to run and hide in the nearest foxhole.

My dad must have been chained to the walls of Greek tradition, as in "You married her, so buck up and bear the consequences." And that he did, as her behavior cost him his dream job and left their relationship in tatters.

Mother conducted a frontal attack on the wife of the chairman of the Lewistown school board with her "You must believe in Jesus" and "Do this, this, and this." The chairman retaliated by writing a scathing letter to the Minnesota State Athletic Association, which nixed Dad's forthcoming appointment as statewide athletic director.

Instead of setting boundaries, Dad chose avoidance. He no longer spent any free time with Mother. I became his boy and surrogate wife. I was his companion at all athletic events, professional, college, and high school. He directed his conversation to me at the dinner table.

No wonder Mother hated me more and more.

Dad reluctantly accepted a two-year consolation job as superintendent of schools for Windom, a small town in the southwest corner of Minnesota, population 3,690. Next, he chose to become the assistant superintendent of schools when we moved to the Minneapolis area in 1958, which meant he no longer reported directly to the school board. He also made sure we lived in a different suburb (Robbinsdale) than where he worked in Fridley. He was determined to limit Mother's ability to affect his career.

Avoidance. No boundaries. Not the best example for his children.

## BOUNDARIES ARE TANGIBLE

A boundary is a clear line. It tells us where to stop. It defines where one thing ends and another begins. In any relationship, boundaries define where things like our personhood, our identity, our responsibility, and our control begin and end, relative to the other person. Sounds cut and dried, and maybe even easy to do, but seeing and understanding relationship boundaries is a blurry, fuzzy, and at times contradictory process!

Setting and maintaining boundaries is even more complicated. Lots of factors are involved on multiple levels: physical, emotional, mental, and spiritual. Family dynamics of our childhood set the stage and determine the opening lines for our adult interactions. Our learned behaviors might include codependency, enmeshment, or avoidance (or discernment, if we got lucky!—some people have the innate ability to perceive, understand, and judge things clearly, especially things not obvious or straightforward):

- *Codependency:* Most psychologists and therapists describe codependency as an "addiction to a relationship." A codependent person will do anything to maintain the status quo in the relationship. They tend to cater to the needs of the other person while ignoring or disregarding their own needs.
- *Enmeshment:* Someone in an enmeshed relationship is overly connected and is so compelled to meet the other person's needs that "they lose touch with their own needs, goals, desires, and feelings," explains Debra Roberts, a clinical licensed social worker. "Often, just the thought of being without the person can be anxiety-producing."[2]
- *Avoidance:* Adults with an avoidant-dismissive insecure attachment style are the opposite of those who are ambivalent or anxious-preoccupied. Instead of craving intimacy, they're so wary of closeness that they try to avoid emotional connection with others. They'd rather not rely on others or have others rely on them.

---

2   Simone Marie, "What Are Enmeshed Relationships? And How to Set Boundaries," PsychCentral, updated July 30, 2021, https://psychcentral.com/lib/tips-on-setting-boundaries-in-enmeshed-relationships#what-are-they.

As the imaginary professor asks for a show of hands from those exhibiting this third behavior, my hand is sheepishly raised in the back of the lecture hall.

## BREAKING BOUNDARY BARRIERS

Boundaries are a bedrock of self-care. They help us take care of our mental health and ensure that our well-being is respected.

Alyssa Mairanz, LMHC, DBTC, advises us to first identify what myths we have regarding boundaries. In her blog series "Overcoming Barriers to Setting Boundaries," she says that we need to gain a clear understanding of our myths, which will help explain what keeps us from advocating for ourselves.[3]

Myths That Compromise Self-Care:

◆ **Myth #1:** "Other peoples' needs are more important than mine."

Hogwash! Some people influence more people than others, but no one has more right to your sanctity of being than you. As we can see on Brenda MacIntyre's website Medicine Song Woman, Indigenous wisdom from elders teaches that "when you make yourself top priority, you open up so much more space within yourself, and your ability to hold space for others opens up too."[4]

My sisters and I were repeatedly told that the biggest sin of all is the "I" in the middle of the word. Recognition for good performance = sin of pride. Recognition for being innovative and creative = sin of disobedience. Striving to achieve results or possessions = sin of envy.

---

3   Alyssa Mairanz, "Overcoming Barriers to Setting Boundaries," EYMT Therapy, April 23, 2018, https://eymtherapy.com/blog/barriers-to-setting-boundaries/.

4   Brenda MacIntyre, "How to Be Supportive without Feeling Drained: Indigenous Wisdom that Changed My Life," Medicine Song Woman, accessed September 23, 2024, https://medicinesongwoman.com/how-to-be-supportive-without-feeling-drained.

It's tough to value yourself when you are shamed for achieving or performing. Shaming is the real sin. It sends the message that you are not worthy. It demeans and shows disdain.

- **Myth #2:** "I don't deserve to get what I need or want."

Not true. You deserve to be heard. Speak up for what you need. Call upon your wise woman sisterhood to give you courage and hold your hand. Stand tall and try not to cringe.

You know your story. You know the adversities you have overcome, the challenges you have grown through. Think about your successes. You are resilient. You are still standing. You have the right to get what you need. You are worthy.

- **Myth #3:** "Setting this boundary will lead to conflict that I cannot handle."

Take time to breathe, and then stop catastrophizing. As Alyssa Mairanz assures us, the feared consequence of setting a boundary is generally worse than the actual outcome. Get clear on what your fear is, i.e., confrontation, conflict, the person getting mad. Ask yourself how likely that outcome is. Ask what would happen if it did; what's the worst result possible, and how you would deal with the consequences? Visualizing positive next steps is incredibly powerful.

## Wisdom Under Pressure

> Josie's mother had mental health issues, her father was an abusive alcoholic, and she was changing diapers and feeding hungry babies by the time she was four. Her father beat her whenever her six siblings misbehaved. He figured since she was the oldest, she was responsible for their behavior. By the time she was twelve, she was the primary target of her father's rage. Determined to escape,

Josie started to babysit and clean houses as soon as she could convince someone to hire her. She graduated from high school with honors, landing scholarships to several colleges, and managed to complete one year of school before her father found out. Furious that money was being wasted on a girl, he refused to sign any financial aid documents.

Defeated and deflated, Josie was forced to drop out and did what she was conditioned to do. She caved into the demands of a violent drug addict in hopes of gaining safety and a modicum of affection and was soon pregnant. Shortly after her son was born, the drug addict left, and an abusive, alcoholic husband, Mike, took his place. Another pregnancy, another baby, more abuse. One night, in a drunken rage, Mike beat Josie so badly that she needed emergency medical care. Instead of calling an ambulance, Mike locked her in the bedroom for three days until she had to go to work. As soon as she escaped from the house, Josie called Al-Anon, the support group for family members of an alcoholic.

Josie hit the jackpot when Spike volunteered to be her sponsor. Spike taught her how to set boundaries and focus on her own behavior instead of trying to change Mike's: No excuses. Stop being a doormat. Learn to effectively use your voice.

AA's Serenity Prayer became Josie's mantra: "God grant me the serenity to accept the things I cannot change, the courage to change the things I can, and the wisdom to know the difference." Eventually Josie convinced Mike to attend AA meetings, but he was one of those guys who stops drinking and becomes a dry drunk. It took years for Josie to gain the strength and courage to leave Mike. Al-Anon remained her lifeline, and Alateen became her children's haven as soon as they were old enough to join.

With Spike's help and a zillion Al-Anon meetings, Josie's confidence grew as she became mentally healthy. She went back to college, finished her undergraduate degree, and was accepted into an occupational therapist program. Josie now had the courage to leave Mike and the strength to work her way through school as a single mom. Sadly, Mike stalked and harassed her and refused to pay child support. But Josie and her kids survived. Eventually, she was able to recoup back child support and buy a safe home of her own. Today, Josie describes herself as one of the happiest people she knows.

### BOUNDARIES ALL AROUND

We encounter multiple types of boundaries in our lives, so be prepared:

- *Physical boundaries provide a foundation.*

    Women are not as strong as men. We may be quicker, but we do not have the muscle mass or physical strength to prevent males from overpowering us. We need healthy physical boundaries. They are the basis for self-care. Vigilance—being alert to physical intrusion, planning ahead, learning martial arts, choosing your environment carefully—gives you an edge. Escaping from the house my mother controlled by boarding the train from Minneapolis to Seattle when I was seventeen allowed me to establish my first physical boundary.

- *Emotional boundaries maintain our individuality.*

    Emotional boundaries are vital in order to know what is and isn't ours to feel or fix. Our emotions and emotional well-being are within our control regardless of what is happening for the other person. Emotional boundaries can mean not letting our own mood be contingent on the mood of our teenager or partner. We all have our own thoughts and feelings, and it is possible to care about each other without losing our sense of self.

Red alert! Verbal abuse and emotional intimidation violate our right to psychological sanctity. It's inappropriate for others to ask certain things of us. We have the right to say no.

◆ *Intellectual boundaries broaden our thinking.*

Everyone has different beliefs, ideas, and values. Don't expect people in your relationships to share all your opinions or adopt all your views. Intellectual boundaries give us freedom. And it feels better to remain true to our beliefs than to acquiesce and "be good."

One spectacular autumn day when I was fifteen and still living at home, my dad was lecturing me as we approached the picturesque overlook of Taylors Falls, on the border of Minnesota and Wisconsin. When he started hammering the steering wheel to emphasize that it was my "duty" to be nice to my mother, my moment of clarity struck.

I turned to him and said succinctly, "She is not my mother. A real mother would never be this abusive to her child. The only way I can tolerate being in the same house as her is to view her as a random woman you married."

The moment I said this to my dad, I felt an iron wall slam down, protecting me from her. From then on, I was able to think of Mother as the woman married to my dad, not my mother. Dad was mortified. I was thrilled. I had just set my first clear boundary. She no longer had the power to influence how I valued *me*. The word "Mother" became just a name for Dad's wife. That was it. I was no longer duty-bound to her.

Forty years later, I finally cleared the trauma she caused from my being. While participating in the trauma track at Sierra Tucson, I was able to "rewrite" my frequent dream of being a terrified little girl who snuck out of bed to confront the bogeyman in my pink flannel nightgown. The recurrent dream would always stop with me frozen in place when the bogeyman, swathed in white athletic wraps, squatted down in front of me, eye to eye. The new script had me saved by a big, powerful leopard who let me climb on his back. The leopard slogged through the muck surrounding me and magically carried me to the top of the tallest tree on a remote island in the middle of the Atlantic Ocean. This imaginary treetop became my first "safe" place.

The final cords binding me to Mother were severed during a psychodrama toward the end of my stay at Sierra Tucson. I was prompted to visualize a sequence of events that rescued me (as a fetus) from my mother's womb. The idea that she had given physical birth to me was so abhorrent that I had to erase it at the cellular level. I had intellectually forgiven her twenty years earlier, but my body and soul still remembered the pain. At the age of fifty-six, the last emotional cords were cut, the last vestiges of baggage were dropped, and I was able to move on.

For the first fifty-six years of my life, I was a master of avoidance rather than a student of my wise woman within. I actually escaped to Africa to avoid being in a relationship with my second husband, not having the courage to confront and advocate for myself.

# D R E A M:
*Saying No and Setting Boundaries*

**D**esire: Advocate with courage for myself.

**R**eflect on when, where, and with whom I feel comfortable enough to say no.

**E**xplore safe places and situations where I can practice setting boundaries.

**A**cknowledge that I have an unalienable right as a human being to say no.

**M**antra:
Give me clarity to understand my needs,
Wisdom to know my limits,
And courage to use my voice.

## WISE WOMAN WORDS

"Choose YOU and be selective of who gets your attention, time, and energy."
–Brenda MacIntyre, Medicine Song Woman

# 3

# Forgiving Yourself and Others

When someone important to us says, "Please forgive me. I didn't mean to hurt you or slight you or cause you pain," we may respond, "Yes, I forgive you," when we really want to say, "Hell no. It's not fair for you to walk away unpunished. You need to suffer, just like you made me suffer." This vindictiveness is natural, but truthfully, the opposite happens. When we don't forgive, *we* suffer. We are the ones stuck in anger and resentment. The other person may experience feelings of guilt, but that is their issue to deal with, not ours. For us to move forward and grow, that piece of emotional baggage needs to be dropped now, never to be picked back up.

"We don't need to pardon or dismiss the offense," according to Kim Cameron, author of *Positive Leadership: Strategies for Extraordinary Performance*. "Acknowledge and reframe negative feelings and attitudes."[5] Forgiveness does not mean condoning what was done. It means taking what happened seriously and not minimizing it—drawing out the sting in the memory that threatens to poison our entire existence.

Forgiveness is not weak, cowardly, or a retreat. As Mahatma Gandhi so eloquently stated, "The weak can never forgive. Forgiveness is the

---

5  Kim Cameron, *Positive Leadership: Strategies for Extraordinary Performance* (Berrett-Koehler Publishers, 2012).

attribute of the strong." When someone that matters to us says or does something that makes us feel diminished or disrespected, we have a choice: to take the easy way out and allow their behavior to make us feel like a victim or to stand tall, draw on our strength, and move forward.

Desmond Tutu offers a wonderful explanation in his book *No Future Without Forgiveness*: "Forgiving and being reconciled are not about pretending that things are other than they are. It is not patting one another on the back and turning a blind eye to the wrong. True reconciliation exposes the awfulness, the abuse, the pain, the degradation, the truth."[6] It involves trying to understand the perpetrator.

In the previous two chapters, I talked about the profound influence my mother's behavior had on me. It has taken time, but I finally understand *why* she behaved the way she did. She was the youngest girl of seven children born to a poor German farming family in South Dakota in 1916. Her father died before I was born, but I knew her mother, Amanda Kruse. During the nineteen years I was required to do chores for her, I don't recall ever hearing Grandma Kruse say a nice word about anybody. She hated everyone, particularly my father. She was bitter, controlling, and never showed appreciation.

Addiction was my mother's coping mechanism. First to card games and then to religion. I doubt if she ever wanted to be a mother. She was kind to other people, so I assume she meant to treat me and my sisters well. But she didn't have a clue about what healthy parenting looked like. She had a poor role model. I was rebellious, and she couldn't make me obey. The only way she could make sense of my behavior was to pretend I wasn't her daughter, which meant I became the "devil's child."

## THE IMMIGRANT

My dad, Jim Pappas, had quite a different story. It started in a Greek/Turkish border town in 1914 during the Balkan Wars. His father,

---

6  Desmond Tutu, *No Future Without Forgiveness* (Image, 2000).

Georgis Papazeus, was forced to forsake his true love and marry my grandma, Sultana. She was ten years younger, short, and not very pretty. Georgis attempted to escape the arranged marriage by joining the Greek merchant marines. Fate prevailed, however, and several years later, when Georgis's ship returned to port, his father whisked him off to Thessaloniki as soon as his boots hit Greek soil. The ceremony took place, the marriage was consummated, and Georgis immediately fled the scene, hiring on to another ship. He jumped that ship in New York City, responded to an ad for railroad workers in far-off South Dakota, and attempted to live a bachelor's life.

Across the Atlantic, the Balkan conflicts continued, and Grandma Sultana was forced to flee with her ten-day-old infant son, my dad. Somehow, they managed to safely settle with extended family on the island of Corfu, more than 500 miles away. In 1921, Georgis decided that he needed his wife and used his meager savings to book passage for eighteen-year-old Grandma Sultana and five-year-old Demetrius (Dad) to cross the Atlantic on a crowded immigrant transport ship. When the two of them were being processed on Ellis Island, the immigration official arbitrarily decided that dad's name should be James Pappas instead of Demetrius Papazeus!

My dad managed to play a remarkable game of life with the hand of cards he was dealt. He grew up in the tiny town of Butler, South Dakota. His parents never spoke English. Bullies routinely beat him on his way to and from school and ridiculed him for his lack of English and odd-looking clothes. Dad survived. In fact, he thrived! Not only was he able to work his way through college, earning an undergrad degree in history, but he also forged ahead and got his master's in school administration while supporting his wife and small daughters.

By the time our family moved to Robbinsdale, Minnesota, in 1958, Dad had saved enough money to buy a twenty-unit motel. He worked as the assistant superintendent and curriculum coordinator for the Fridley school system during the day and ran the motel at night, scrubbing the bathrooms of all the units every Sunday, convinced that the maids were taking shortcuts. He acquired four apartment buildings over the next few years, always checking and rechecking that the apartment managers met his standards. Dad worked and worked, and when he had spare time, he took me, his preferred companion, to baseball, football, and basketball games.

Dad inherited that unfortunate avoidance trait from his father, which he later passed on to his girls. When his emotions became conflicted and confused, he retreated. His father physically escaped to America when he was denied marriage to his sweetheart. Dad escaped through work, managing the motel and apartments and planting and transplanting trees. He was emotionally unavailable. He wanted peace and was willing to do anything to make the noise stop.

## SUICIDE BY RAGE

My dad had many wonderful traits. He excelled at his job and was beloved by school district employees, including principals, teachers, janitors, cooks, and bus drivers. He was a well-respected boss, kind and fair, who worked tirelessly and overcame early obstacles of poverty, learned English, and coped with being an outsider. The flip side? He bottled up his emotions, and whenever the lid blew off, the explosion was epic!

Appearances mattered a lot to Dad, so it was important that we looked like the "all-American family." My sisters were willing to dress the part, but not me. One summer day, on a road trip to Somewhere, USA, we stopped to take a walk through a large park. My sister Eileen and I were walking in front of our parents when a kid yelled out while pointing directly at me, "Hey, Mom, look! There's a beatnik."

Dad erupted! He rushed us back to our 1955 Chrysler and shoved Eileen and me into the back seat, tires squealing as he peeled out of the parking lot. Dad's arms flailed as he swatted at me while we swerved down the road. Absolutely apoplectic, red-faced, sweat running down his cheeks, with mother shrieking, me huddled against the car door to evade his slaps, and Eileen screaming.

That night in the motel room, Mother frantically cut off the tails of my men's shirts and hand-sewed waist-length hems. I was furious. It had taken months for me to save up my fifty-cent weekly allowance to buy those shirts.

The evening my dad came close to strangling my mother (described in chapter 1) was also traumatic, but I believe the rage my dad bottled up against Ted Haider was what killed him.

After Dad sold his apartment buildings, a businessman named Ted Haider sold him a building on West Broadway in Minneapolis that was leased as a bowling alley. It turned out to be a bad business deal, and Dad lost money. Instead of accepting that he had made a mistake, Dad blamed Mr. Haider. Not passively. Vehemently. One day shortly before my dad died of a massive stroke, he was having dinner with my family when his face turned red, sweat running down his cheeks, but there were no words or waving of the arms—just bottled rage with no way to defuse his turmoil and no place to escape. Not being able to forgive and move on eventually killed him.

My former stepdaughter Leah put things into perspective for me by sharing an old adage: "Holding a grudge is like drinking poison and expecting the other person to die."

She's right. Nothing good comes from it. Refusing to forgive often causes depression, irritability, and anxiety. Grudges create bottlenecks to forming new healthy relationships. And for people who have high blood pressure like my dad, bottled anger can be deadly.

## **EVERYONE HAS SOMEONE TO FORGIVE**

At some point, everyone has been hurt by the actions or words of another person. Critical parents. Sabotaging colleagues. Partners who have affairs. Perhaps you have suffered physical or emotional abuse by someone close to you. These wounds can leave lasting resentment, bitterness, and anger, and sometimes even hatred.

By embracing forgiveness, we can also embrace peace and hope. Of course, forgiveness means different things to different people. Generally, forgiveness involves an intentional decision to let go of resentment and anger. We may always remember the act that hurt us, but we can lessen its grip. We have the power to free ourselves from the control of the people who harmed us. It doesn't mean forgetting or excusing the harm done, and we certainly don't have to "make up" with the person who caused the harm. However, forgiveness gives us the ability to focus on ourselves and helps us move on with our lives.

Twenty-six years after Dad died, I wrote him a letter while at Sierra Tucson, sharing the impact his decisions had on my life. I doubt if he would have understood what I was talking about had he been alive to read the letter. Much of the vocabulary we use today wasn't commonplace in the 1970s, such as having a voice, the importance of touch, advocating the sanctity of the child, the impact of being told conflicting messages, the importance of trust, and feeling safe enough to allow vulnerability. I had to understand him to be able to forgive his failure to protect me.

As a result, I became a healthier me. My mental health improved. I felt less anxiety, stress, and hostility. Lower blood pressure. A stronger immune system. Improved heart health. Better self-esteem. I benefited from letting go! In fact, forgiveness provided freedom.

By letting go of old grudges and bitterness, I had more space to welcome peace, happiness, and emotional and spiritual healing. I was able to reclaim power from the people who wronged me.

## FORGIVING YOURSELF IS AN UPHILL CLIMB

It was easier for me to forgive others than to forgive myself for being a subpar mom versus a supermom. I worked so hard to overachieve and to be everything I wish my mother had been that I ended up failing with the basics. I was too tired to be emotionally available. I became a gerbil running on a perpetually spinning wheel. For years, I felt responsible whenever one of my kids made unhealthy or disappointing choices.

Why was it so hard to forgive myself for making mistakes as a mom? According to Georgia Lepenioti, MSC, who practices psychology in Europe, "Every time we act in a way we feel is wrong, we create a cognitive dissonance. When we act against our ethical values, we feel an internal disconnect, which makes us feel the need to do something to fix the 'wrong.' Since it is impossible to delete our actions, we start punishing ourselves for them. Harmful, self-directed behaviors that happen consciously or unconsciously hinder our self-forgiveness."[7]

There are a number of tough obstacles to conquer in forgiving ourselves:

- *Obstacle #1: Negative Self-Talk*

    Dwelling on situations and making ourselves feel worse will halt any progress in self-forgiveness. Instead of focusing on the wrong behavior and planning to correct it, we keep judging and deriding ourselves as if we were our worst enemy. Why not reframe what happened and try to think of it as a learning experience?

- *Obstacle #2: Rumination*

    According to Edward R. Watkins, PhD, professor of experimental and applied clinical psychology at the University of Exeter, "Rumination involves repetitive thinking or dwelling on negative feelings and distress and their causes and consequences."[8] We keep "reliving" our mistakes in our minds, over and over. As a result, we beat ourselves up, feel guilt

---

[7] Georgia Lepenioti, MSC, "Self-Forgiveness—Why Is It So Hard?" GoodTherapy, June 7, 2023, https://www.goodtherapy.org/blog/welf-forgiveness-why-is-it-so-hard/.

[8] "Rumination: A Cycle of Negative Thinking," American Psychiatric Association, March 5, 2020, https://www.psychiatry.org/news-room/apa-blogs/rumination-a-cycle-of-negative-thinking.

and shame, and get stuck in a vicious circle.

Replaying what we did in our heads isn't going to help us or the person we hurt. It just makes us feel bad. So, every time you catch yourself ruminating on your sins, stop! Refocus your attention on something more positive. Tell yourself that whatever happened does *not* define who you are.

Most importantly, rumination interferes with effective problem-solving. When we focus repeatedly on negative feelings and thoughts, we aren't able to accept the situation and forgive ourselves. Our own cognitive biases, the unhelpful thinking habits that we have developed during our lives, hinder the process of self-forgiveness.

- *Obstacle #3: Those Darn "Supposed-Tos"*

Many of us have the self-sabotaging habit of second-guessing ourselves based on external pressures. "I should have done this" or "I shouldn't have said that."

We might think that a supermom should be able to do this and that and everything in between and still have the mind space to be emotionally available and the time to sit quietly, 100 percent focused on her children. Why buy into the role of supermom? Not possible for a mere human being.

## SELF-COMPASSION IS THE ANSWER

According to a meta-analysis of self-forgiveness conducted by Georgia Lepenioti, MSC, in the Netherlands, forgiveness of self is positively related to psychological well-being and life satisfaction.[9] It reduces feelings of shame and self-punishment without excusing our behavior. Individuals who forgive themselves still take responsibility for their actions but have fewer feelings of shame and self-condemnation.

Author Ellen Michaud quotes Dr. Fred Luskin, senior consultant

---

9   Lepenioti, "Self-Forgiveness—Why Is It So Hard?"

in health promotion and wellness at Stanford University and director of the Stanford University Forgiveness Project, on the topic of forgiveness in her article "12 Ways to Forgive Yourself for a Past Mistake": "Forgiveness is a tool with which we face what we've done in the past, acknowledge our mistakes, and move on. It does not mean that you condone or excuse what happened. It does not mean that you forget. . . . There's a season for our suffering and regret. We have to have that. But the season ends; the world moves on. And we need to move on with it."[10]

## STEP 1: SELF-KINDNESS

Treat yourself like you would your best friend. Apply a caring rather than judgmental attitude toward your personal failures. Don't punish yourself by feeling miserable for the rest of your life. Michaud explains Dr. Luskin's view: "Some of us try to use those bad feelings like a talisman to ward off the consequences of our actions, says Dr. Luskin. We curl up in a ball and say, 'Hey! Look how bad I feel! See how I'm suffering! I'm pitiful! I'm pathetic! I can't be punished any more than this—it wouldn't be fair!'"[11]

Rather than take this route, take responsibility for what you have done by determining realistic ways to repair the damage or make things right. It's much healthier to replace your inner critic with a more realistic and encouraging coach!

## STEP 2: SELF-ACCEPTANCE

It is human to make mistakes. You were not designated at birth to be the only perfect person in the world. You are just like all the rest of us: *flawed*. Accept your flaws as part of you.

Most of us do the best we can, even when we hurt someone—even when we're too stubborn, ashamed, or in denial to admit the hurt we've caused. Even when we have been thoughtless, insensitive, and selfish, we

---

10  Research by Dr. Fred Luskin referenced in Ellen Michaud, "12 Ways to Forgive Yourself for a Past Mistake," Ellen Michaud, February 13, 2019, http://ellenmichaud.com/forgiveyourself.html.
11  Michaud, "12 Ways to Forgive Yourself."

usually have good intentions. We're doing the best we know how to do.

Acceptance does not mean that we justify our wrong behavior. It just means that we accept our imperfections and try to understand our mistakes so that we can grow from them. Most of us have a set of unconscious rules hovering in the backs of our minds about how we expect ourselves to behave. But those rules, many of which we absorbed in childhood and never really thought about, are not always realistic.

### Compost Happens

Diana Dean's mother died in an auto accident when she was thirteen years old. Diana was instantly thrust into the role of caregiver for her four younger siblings. Her father's routine physical and emotional abuse escalated, and Diana became the number one target. Although she physically left home as soon as she was able, the emotional hot spots and triggers traveled with her for decades, and eventually three unsatisfactory marriages ended in divorce.

Diana searched extensively for answers to the question "Why me?" She earned a doctor of psychology degree. Later, during therapy, Diana discovered that the abuse she suffered was not about her; it was about the demons from her father's past. As her self-respect and self-value grew, Diana came to understand her father's behavior and was able to compassionately forgive him. After she finally dropped the shameful load of "I am only worthy of abuse," she was able to flourish and grow.

Diana has written a book, *Compost Happens*, which encourages others to gain freedom from their pasts and become their authentic selves. Her favorite saying is "Out of the muck of the past blooms the lotus."

## FORGIVENESS, INDIGENOUS STYLE

In 2007, I started working in the extreme southwestern corner of Ethiopia, the South Omo Valley, home to eight Indigenous tribes: Hamar, Bena, Mursi, Suri, Kara, Dassanech, Arbore, and Nyangatom. They are some of the most fascinating, fearless survivors of impossibly difficult living conditions. (The adventures that landed me in Africa are discussed in later chapters.)

The first initiative I undertook was to distribute free medicine. I needed an entry point into their community in order to build relationships and gain permission to survey their needs. More than 86 percent of the people suffered from intestinal parasites at that point, and a daily dose of mebendazole for a week was an easy fix. I purchased the medicine in Addis Ababa and stuffed hundreds of packages in my black duffel bag to distribute to target communities during the trek to South Omo.

One morning, prior to leaving for the field, Bayu—my driver—and I hurriedly packed the truck. I thought Bayu had grabbed the medicine bag from the closet, but the English-to-Amharic translation was spotty at best. When we unloaded in the field, it started to rain, so we staged all the luggage and food supplies on a tarp while we frantically erected the tents. Hundreds of people crowded around to watch us. When we discovered that the medicine bag was missing, a little boy, Wuchele, said he saw a young Hamar man named Kole take the bag. The elders believed Wuchele and took Kole into custody for five days. They felt that Wuchele had no reason to lie, so Kole must be guilty. Marmaru, the Hamar shaman, flipped his sandals to receive divine guidance from Hamar spirit guides, their ancestors. After five days, Marmaru was not convinced that Kole was guilty, so the elders released him.

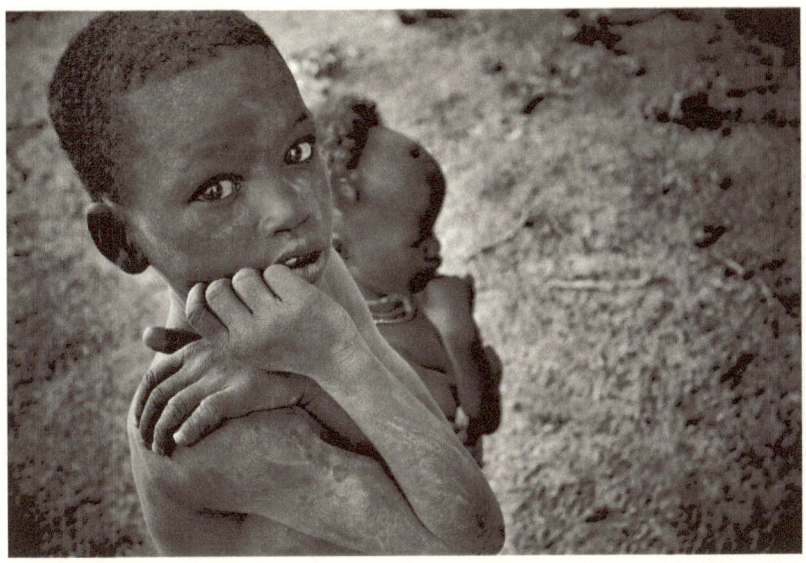

*Wuchele, a young Hamar orphan who mistakenly accused Kole of taking our medicine bag.*

When Bayou and I returned to Addis, we discovered the medicine bag still in my closet. I was devastated. We contacted Emnet, the current Hamar woreda (a woreda is a large county) administrator, for advice. Emnet advised that we wait until I was able to return to Hamar to tell the community that I had made a mistake by claiming the bag had been taken and that Kole had been falsely accused.

The first thing I did when we arrived back in the field was to request a meeting with the elders and Kole. We gathered under the big tree in the sandy riverbed. I told the community what had happened and that I wanted to make amends. The elders and Kole talked and talked. After lengthy discussion I was told, "No worries. You are a human being, and human beings make mistakes." The elders and Kole agreed that I needed to pay Kole approximately $100 for the livestock he had lost during his imprisonment.

*Hamar discussing my punishment for disrupting the harmony of their tribe.*

Then, everyone stood and faced west. Kole and I held hands at the front of the group. In unison, we all took four steps forward, and voilà, I was forgiven, and everyone was happy. No grudges. No penalties. Everyone and everything were once again in harmony. Kole gave me a goat to show he had no hard feelings for my mistake. Several years later, he became an erga (community teacher), and we paid him to help with our projects.

I think that was the moment when I really understood the profound wisdom of these uneducated, highly civilized people. Imagine how different today's world would be if globally and collectively we focused on harmony versus greed and power.

We have much to learn from these wise people. They never carry emotional baggage. When they forgive, the issue is over. They are filled with wisdom to share—if our minds are open, willing to listen and observe.

# DREAM:
## *Forgiving Myself and Others*

**D**esire: Drop my emotional baggage so I become free to grow faster.

**R**eflect on the fears that prevent me from forgiving myself and others.

**E**xplore the resentments and feelings of "If only I had done this or that" dragging me down.

**A**cknowledge that I am not perfect, and neither is anyone else.

**M**antra:
Forgive. Let Go. Move On.
Release the pain of betrayal.
Exhale the bitterness.
Inhale self-acceptance.
Reclaim my power and heal.

### WISE WOMAN WORDS

"I forgive you for not being the way I wanted you to be.
I forgive you and set you free."
—Linda Hey

# 4

# Being the Curious Entrepreneur of Your Own Life

During my time in San Francisco, while living in a barren bedroom with a shared toilet down the hall at the age of seventeen, an epiphany left me gobsmacked. I was looking out over the rooftops of the neighboring row houses one night, feeling cold and lonely, when I realized there was an *advantage* to having been emotionally and mentally gutted in the nuthouse and forbidden to live at home. Since I was an empty shell, I could fill myself up the way I wanted. I could determine *my* values, *my* belief system, and what I was going to accomplish in life. It was up to me to become who I wanted to be.

I viewed my go-forward life as a blank canvas awaiting transformation into a picture that I had to paint. My time with my birth family was over. It was old news. My future was full of variables I could influence. Somehow, someway, without a role model or a traditional support system, I needed to define how I wanted to live my life, and then build it, brick by brick, step by step.

The folk singers of the sixties became my imaginary support team. I listened to their songs every night, over and over. Lyrics like those from Joan Baez's "Forever Young" and Glen Yarborough's "Baby the Rain Must Fall" helped me dream of possibilities. I recommend you give those a listen.

## FISH OUT OF WATER

I formed a vision of who I wanted *me* to be—financially independent, safe, and *not* bored. My strongest motivator was curiosity. I wanted to learn, to experience, to feel free, but I wasn't equipped to succeed. I was underage, and I had no access to money and no support mechanism other than my father. I realized that until I could earn enough money to be independent, Dad ultimately called the shots, and my options were limited.

I have always been a seeker of truth. My first memory of being curious began in my parents' bedroom at Grandma Pappas's house when I tried to decipher images on the wallpaper surrounding my iron crib. That cool, old-fashioned wallpaper told simple stories through a combination of words and pictures. I learned to read there, amusing myself while trapped alone each afternoon.

My love for problem-solving showed up early as well. I could assemble the forty-eight-state USA puzzle faster than anyone in my family. I loved doing puzzles, figuring out how things fit together spatially instead of mechanically.

One December day at work in San Francisco, I met a girl in the JCPenney cafeteria who wanted to move to Los Angeles and start at the University of California there in January. We planned to fly to LA as soon as I returned from an obligatory Christmas week in Minneapolis, which was my payment for permission to stay in San Francisco as a seventeen-year-old.

During the holiday, I applied to UCLA and was promptly accepted, as I had aced my college entrance exams prior to losing my photographic memory. I managed to convince my dad to allow me to attend. The girl in San Francisco, however, changed her mind, so unbeknownst to Dad, I traveled to LA by myself.

Sixteen months earlier, in August 1965, the Watts riots, among the bloodiest, costliest, and most analyzed uprisings of the notoriously unsettled mid-1960s, occurred ten miles from LAX. The six-day upheaval resulted in thirty-four deaths, more than 3,400 arrests, and tens of millions of dollars in property damage. It was certainly no place for an underage Midwestern girl to wander around alone. When I got off the plane, I had absolutely no idea where UCLA was located. There I was, standing on the curb outside the arrivals at one of the world's busiest airports, with all my worldly possessions in two suitcases. My sister Willow helped me out once again. She knew a guy who agreed to pick me up and help me rent a tiny efficiency apartment a few blocks from campus.

The day before classes started, I made the mistake of calling my dad, who was furious to learn that I had moved to LA by myself. I failed to convince him that I was safer alone than with "no-name stranger girl," but no success. He gave me an ultimatum: either attend California Lutheran Bible School (CLBS), where Dad was a supporter, or return home. There was no way I was going to live under the same roof as my mother, so I chose the Bible school.

Being seventeen really sucked.

CLBS was near McArthur Park in downtown LA, a hotbed of "free love and pot" in the mid-'60s, which sounded exciting. The CLBS teachers, however, were narrow-minded, and the kids were holy rollers. I made sure to show my disdain by wearing miniskirts, excessive eye makeup, Beatle bangs, and dangling earrings.

## FEELING MY OATS

Seeking a part-time job to advance my journey toward independence while attending the Bible school, I was immediately hired for a three-day job at Hayward Tamkin Mortgage Bankers. When they were impressed with how I reorganized the downstairs filing system, I was transferred to accounting, where I met my new best friend, Linda Featherstone.

Linda and I spent our free time getting drunk and driving to the ocean in her dilapidated 1956 Chevy. The car's undercarriage had rusted through, and the back seat had no floorboards. Our feet could touch the interstate while we barreled along at high speeds. We partied every moment we were not at work or in school. We slept on the beach, drove up to Mount Wilson for snowball fights, and hung out on the Sunset Strip. Hanging out with Linda gave me my first feeling of being unfettered and free.

In March 1967, Phil Salewski, the US marine brother of a boy I dated for a minute in Seattle, was transferred to Camp Pendleton, just south of LA, for deployment to Vietnam. Phil and I had been corresponding since his brother dumped me. He came to LA on weekends to hang out. When Pastor Force, the head of CLBS, discovered I was seeing Phil unchaperoned, he summoned me to his office to expel me from school. Unfortunately, he changed his mind when he saw my huge grin. *Darn.* I hated CLBS with every fiber in my being. I just wanted to work and earn enough money to go to college.

Finally, my eighteenth birthday arrived, and I put my rudimentary plan into action. I fumbled and stumbled and had a tough time making ends meet. I managed to attend LA City College part-time while working full-time, quickly learning that I had no idea what success looked like. I knew what I didn't like but had no clue what would make me happy and fulfilled. Looking back, if I had been less rebellious, stubborn, and bloody independent, my journey to finding a sense of peace would have been smoother, and much quicker.

When I first tried to visualize the life I wanted, I had no concept of what paths or options were available. I just knew I needed a challenge. I hated wasting time doing stupid stuff but didn't have the wisdom to ascertain importance. And I didn't like to take direction from people I didn't respect, so I either needed to pick good leaders or become a leader myself.

## INSPIRED BY BROWNIES

When I was seven years old, I had a chance to learn from the wisdom of others during my brief tenure as a Brownie, also known as an elementary-age Girl Scouts. True to form, it took only one meeting before I was kicked out for insubordination. If I had been more compliant, I could have taken advantage of their road map to entrepreneurship.

- *Recognize and Celebrate*: Girl Scouts teach girls to recognize and celebrate the great things they are already doing.
- *Acknowledge and Encourage:* Girl Scouts acknowledge and encourage girls to be curious and adapt to a changing environment, collaborate with others, take initiative, and embrace challenges.
- *Skills to Overcome the Fear of Failure*: Girls Scouts teach skills to overcome the fear of failure by making it safe to take risks.
- *Practice Entrepreneurship:* Girl Scouts give girls the opportunities to practice entrepreneurship by learning goal setting, management, people skills, and business ethics.

The opportunity was there, but I didn't see it because I was too focused on getting my own way.

## CHOOSE THE MAGIC OF YES OVER THE CONSEQUENCES OF NO

In *The Path of Least Resistance: Learning to Become the Creative Force in Your Own Life*, author Robert Fritz discusses how we can find inspiration in our own lives that will help us drive the creative process.[12] This can lead us to manifest our deepest desires, and it begins with making several relevant and helpful choices.

---

12  Robert Fritz, *The Path of Least Resistance: Learning to Become the Creative Force in Your Own Life* (Ballantine Books, 1989).

## SAY NO TO...

- *Choice by limitation.* "I want *this*, but, oh well, I guess I can only have *that*. Poor me!"
- *Choice by elimination.* The situation rules. "There was nothing else I could do!" or "I had no choice but to . . . [hit, lie, steal, ignore, take the easy way out, etc.]."
- *Choice by default.* The choice to *not* make a choice. When you don't decide, you choose no.
- *Conditional choice.* "I'll do this *if* this other thing happens or *when* conditions are perfect."
- *Choice by fear of the unknown.* "I will feel bad if *this* happens, so I'll do *that* instead."
- *Choice by consensus.* "This is what everyone tells me to do. I guess I should do it. I don't know, what do you think?"

## SAY YES TO...

- *Creative choice.* Consciously make choices based on what *you* want to see manifested. Creatives do not make choices based on what they don't want. It could be that what you want is the opposite of what you don't want, and that's fine, but the choice is still "what you want."

## LESSONS FROM LEONARDO

Leonardo da Vinci viewed himself as a man of science and engineering rather than as an artist. He was deemed a misfit: illegitimate, gay, vegetarian, easily distracted, and at times heretical. My kind of guy!

Leonardo's genius was forged by his own will and ambition. He had almost no schooling. His brilliance was based on a deep curiosity and devotion to observation.

Joseph Thomas, president and CEO at Freedom Bank and author of "Stay Curious: What Entrepreneurs Can Learn from Da Vinci," relates several nuggets he gleaned from celebrated biographer Walter Isaacson's 2017 book, *Leonardo da Vinci*. Isaacson shows how Leonardo's genius was based on skills we can fine-tune for ourselves, such as passionate curiosity, careful observation, and a playful imagination.

Lesson highlights, including some of my own thoughts:[13]

- "*Be relentlessly curious.*" Curiosity is a mental muscle, and just like any muscle in the body, it needs to be exercised regularly to stay strong. When curiosity flags, stagnation seeps in.
- "*Observe.* Develop an acute ability to observe things . . . [and] wonder why."
- "*Respect facts.* . . . Be fearless about changing [your mind] based on new information." What you think is true today may be wrong tomorrow.
- "*Let your reach exceed your grasp.* Take on the hard problems and accept that there are some issues you may never resolve." Learn from the process of seeking to understand.
- "*Collaborate.* Genius starts with individual brilliance and requires a singular vision, but executing it often entails working with others. Innovation and creativity are collaborative endeavors."
- *Take time to reflect.* "The pace of change is grueling, and competition is so fierce that it's often difficult to make time and space for reflection." To absorb what we learn, we have to reflect.

## MY MODEL FOR SUCCESS

In the early nineties, I was privileged to attend a two-week executive graduate program at Stanford. I was a sponge, soaking up every modicum of advice available. One simple graph that imprinted on my brain and has become an everyday tool depicts Professor Robert

---

13  Joseph Thomas, "Stay Curious: What Entrepreneurs Can Learn from Da Vinci," LinkedIn, Jan 12, 2018, https://www.linkedin.com/pulse/stay-curious-what-entrepreneurs-can-learn-from-da-vinci-joseph-thomas-1/.

Terry's leadership model[14]. It has only five parts, and it works. I use it for episodic events (conversations, fitness and weight loss, etc.) as well as complex endeavors, such as creating marketing plans, structuring proposals, building relationships, etc. Use it 10,000 times. It works.

- *Visualize*: Imagine the goal or objective you want to reach. Picturing where you want to end up is imperative. Ask the question "What does success look like?" Give free rein to your imagination. Keep thinking, refining, doodling around the edges until your success picture is concrete and specific—and somewhat realistic.
- *Power*: An energy source is needed to get your juices flowing. What will motivate you and fuel your determination? How will you create the volition to catapult you toward your goal? What will give you courage and help you overcome any pesky fears?
- *Environment*: You need to understand your current environment *before* you can build a bridge between where you are and where you want to go. This is critical. Identify your starting situation. Do you have the tools? Do you know someone who can mentor and/or support you? What is your starting point? The pluses and the minuses? Don't exaggerate and don't minimize. Be brutally frank and clear-minded.
- *Resources*: This is the "list of stuff (and people) that is needed to succeed" step. Money, new skills, different relationships, employees, etc. Note: Listing the required resources comes *after* you have clearly identified your starting point, your goal is concrete and specific, and you have a power/motivation/volition plan.
- *Structure*: You must create the most efficient structure possible to facilitate the use of resources (stuff, skills, and people). Think of the structure as the framework or inverted funnel that will allow the resources to be leveraged, ignited to provide maximum power and forward movement.

---

14  Work papers from Dr. Terry's Stanford University's Executive Management class in the early 1990s.

## IT'S OKAY TO CHANGE THE PICTURE

Our first picture of success is seldom realistic or achievable. That's okay. Goals can be modified. Just redefine where you want to be based on what you have learned so far during your journey. Reflect on what was accomplished to date and examine the factors that derailed your progress or created bottlenecks.

There is a lot of rich, fertile information to sift through and examine. New skills may be needed or additional resources garnered, or perhaps our perspective needs to shift. Sometimes, our entire approach must change, and our goal or objective may need to be radically altered. No problem. It's healthy to redefine success. I highly recommend it. Moving the bar and sometimes even lowering it will enable us to jump over it, which does wonders for one's self-esteem.

I found redefining success and learning new business skills exhilarating. But I had a tough time applying this method to my personal life. It is a whole new ball game to feel successful as a parent when your children struggle with depression and addiction.

It took years of work to view myself as a successful mother. I finally changed my picture from June Cleaver on the sixties TV show *Leave It to Beaver* to "I did my very best." Therapy helped me realize that since my children are adults, they have the right to their own picture of success. It is no longer my business.

The iconic college basketball coach John Wooden defined success as "peace of mind, which is a direct result of self-satisfaction in knowing you made the effort to do your best to become the best that you are capable of becoming."

Christopher D. Connors, in his article "The First Step Toward Success Is Defining Success for Yourself," says that success is an attitude.[15] Success requires maximum effort. It is a state of mind that

---

[15] Christopher D. Connors, "The First Step Toward Success Is Defining Success for Yourself," Medium, July 21, 2016, https://medium.com/the-mission/the-first-step-toward-success-is-defining-success-for-yourself-92dcfc3dd61c.

can create peace of mind.

My definition is slightly different. I now believe that success is experiencing joy and satisfaction through discovering and fulfilling your purpose in life, which may change over time.

## MY NO-EXCUSES WISE WOMAN HERO

At the end of my forty-day survey trip to South Omo Valley, Ethiopia, in 2008, I was tired and discouraged. I had worked relentlessly to understand what these incredibly marginalized members of the Hamar tribe needed in order to have a chance for a healthy life. The long, hot days, sleepless nights, difficulties with translating multiple languages, and the flies and bees had taken their toll. I was ready to call it quits, go back to the States, and become a passive donor of funds to "worthy causes."

Then I met Gulu Bola and the women of the Minogelti cooperative. The trajectory of the rest of my life changed. In fact, most everything about me changed.

*Gulu Bola, my wise woman hero.*

Gulu's deck of cards was dealt in one of the poorest, most desolate areas of Africa. The land has been soaked by the blood of tribesmen fighting for access to water, wandering hundreds of miles in search of grazing grounds for their meager herds of goats, sheep, and cattle. They have become victims of massive governmental land grabs as powerful people 500 miles away tried to attract foreign business investments. The valley is still a place where women are treated with less respect than a chimpanzee in the field.

Gulu's birth family was unusual for Hamar. Her father, Bola Guda, was a monogamist. (Hamar elders often have four to five wives.) Gulu had two sisters and four brothers, most of whom are now deceased. The boys grew up working in the fields and following livestock. Gulu and her sisters spent their time grinding sorghum, tending the young animals, and walking miles each day to fetch and carry water. No one in the family could read, write, do simple arithmetic, or speak the national language, Amharic. Gulu was married as soon as her menses began. Her father received cattle, sheep, and honey as her bride price.

Gulu started with nothing in a land of virtually no opportunity. Over the course of her journey, she was brutally abused and expelled from her community. She has endured slander and isolation, but she has not let that define her. She defines herself. Today, she reads, writes, and speaks fluent Amharic; she runs a successful rural trading center and is the respected, recognized spokesperson for Indigenous people of Ethiopia. She has even visited the United Nations and met with members of the US Congress. I was standing next to her when she did.

How was Gulu able to do this? She was curious and she was fearless. She built her life brick by brick. She took responsibility and figured out what success looks like for her, in *her* environment. She is now the role model for her family, friends, and tribe.

Stay tuned for more stories about Gulu.

## Stop Waiting and Lead

Megan Genest Tarnow spends most of her time working in the tiny intersection of Quickbooks (QB) accounting systems and nonprofits. QB, the most widely used accounting software for small business, is structured for companies that sell goods and/or services to make money for their owners. Nonprofits don't make money and don't have owners. They depend on grants and donations to do approved charitable work. Every expense needs to be applied to the appropriate source of funds, which have their own set of rules and reporting requirements. Megan's small accounting team is expert at harnessing QB features to process their nonprofit clients' needs.

Megan was looking forward to exchanging ideas and making connections with her peers at the Minnesota Council of Nonprofits conference one year. Unfortunately, the day before the event was to start, a major blizzard roared in and shut the city down. The conference was canceled. Knocked down but not out, Megan heard a voice repeating the same statement in her head, over and over: *Somebody needs to stop waiting for permission and lead.*

There was little hope that QB would ever organize a nonprofit event, so Megan decided to "make her own room" where she could share learning and facilitate connections.

She started a Facebook group, QB for Non-Profits, in 2018. Five years later, the group has more than 10,000 members. Every month, she hosts a "Lunch and Learn" event so experts can educate and members can share. Megan, a member of Intuit's educator network, now has a virtual room that will never be shut down due to inclement weather. She and 10,000 like-minded souls can hang out and share what they know.

## SHIFTING GROUND AHEAD

Taking responsibility is not easy. Just when we think we have it all figured out, the ground shifts. Our lives become chaotic. New players arrive—partners, children, bosses, employees. We may need to challenge the status quo, learn persuasion techniques, take daunting risks to explore new opportunities, and ask for help. As the environment changes, we must adjust to navigate the chaos.

We have the wisdom within us to find balance, chart new paths, clarify intentions, and become the creative architects of our lives. We have the power of choice. We can experience the magic of saying yes.

# DREAM:
## *Being the Curious Entrepreneur of My Life*

**D**esire: Become the architect of my life.

**R**eflect on what I want to be doing and feeling five years from now.

**E**xplore the habits and skills I currently possess that will help me reach my five-year goal.

**A**cknowledge that I will make mistakes and will need multiple "do-overs."

**M**antra:
I choose to be the master of me.
I am my judge and jury here on earth.
I take responsibility for me.

### WISE WOMAN WORDS

"Don't be intimidated by what you don't know.
That can be your greatest strength and ensure that you do things differently from everyone else."
—Sara Blakely

# PART TWO

## Navigate Your Chaos

Marriage. Children. Divorce. Blending Families. Career. Chaos. Help!

How do we juggle everything while we're caught in a middle-aged squeeze? I've always thought of it as a sandwich. Here we are, the meat between two pieces of bread, with the bottom piece representing the needs of our partners and children, which we desperately want to accommodate, and the top piece of bread representing everyone at work and/or elderly parents and extended family. We keep getting squeezed, and people keep taking bites out of us.

It's messy and exhausting, seeing to the needs of others versus our own needs, wants, and desires—at home, at work, and in our community. In my case, it involved dealing with issues of divorce, kids, being a single mom, growing a business, and learning to manage employees and accommodate their needs as well as the concerns of bankers and customers.

The ground keeps shifting under our feet. Nothing seems stable. Chaos is the norm. How will we cope, let alone flourish? We want to make calm, rational decisions. And the ability to assess situations to avoid land mines would certainly be welcome.

Part 2 encourages you to challenge the status quo and explains how to integrate other peoples' needs and perspectives while you're making decisions. It inspires you to embrace uncertainty, to give yourself a chance to grow and learn from others. Remember, you are not alone. Your sisters are standing beside you, ready to hold your hand.

# 5

# Challenging the Status Quo

*What if* bicycle mechanics Orville and Wilbur Wright, who had no formal engineering training, quit trying to fly after years of crashing? Would human flight still be an impossible dream?

*What if* Rosa Parks had not had the courage to refuse to give up her seat to a White man on a bus in Montgomery, Alabama, in 1955? Would Martin Luther King Jr. have had the stage to give his "I Had a Dream" speech, fueling the civil rights movement?

*What if* innovators like J. C. R. Licklider, Vinton Cerf, and Tim Berners-Lee and colleagues had not envisioned a new way of sharing information? Would we still be using the telephone, postal mail, and broadcast media as our only methods of communication instead of the internet?

These are mere snippets of how you and I have benefited from the courage of brave, creative people. Each one faced significant resistance. Their determination and resilience have given us greater access to information, more opportunities, more adventures, and the ability to stay connected to family and friends wherever they may be.

## WHY NOT ME?

Questioning and defying established norms can open the door to opportunity, learning, and making a difference. Intellectually, we know this to be true, but women do have a more difficult path than men. Men are the ones who established the rules, so naturally they have the edge on navigating and breaking through the barriers.

Men have traditionally been in charge. They hunted and we gathered (and cooked and cleaned up and had babies and . . . ). Male bodies are designed to be strong, but ours are designed to do highly complicated stuff. We have an inherent advantage there.

The male brain is compartmentalized. It's programmed to "See musk ox. Kill musk ox." An idea is formed on the right side of the brain and must travel across the cortex chasm on a rope bridge to the left side, where it can become an action. We females, however, have a weblike structure that allows ideas to form on the right side and pop over to the left, all while talking on the phone and keeping our children from doing naughty things to each other. We are born to multitask.

Honestly, the status quo worked in my favor. I went after complicated jobs. Selling computers in the seventies was men's work; as an outlier, I flipped the "wrong sex" philosophy into an advantage and worked on commission. Obviously not a White male, I wasn't in my "supposed-to" role. I was different—an oddity. I learned to ignore snide remarks and insults. My tough lizard skin deflected their arrows.

## A DUBIOUS BEGINNING

My formative years were in the 1950s, when women were not supposed to work outside the home. Real jobs were for men. In school, we took home economics while the boys took shop class. I was required to sew all my clothes (except the ones I stole). My girlfriends talked about going to college for their "MRS" degree.

When I was sixteen and assigned to write an essay describing my goals in life, I wrote about all the things I wanted to do. Travel, learn about different cultures, climb the highest mountain, and swim in the deepest sea. I craved a life of adventure, learning, and discovery. The last line of my essay said, "Of course, the most important thing in my life is to be a good wife and mother!" There it was—that early, formative programming. So, that's what I tried to do for the next thirty years. I don't recall any female role models other than a few women I saw on television who stood up to a man for a moment, only to be put in her place before the next commercial.

As a shy young adult in the late sixties, I started out doing office work, and since I hated inefficiency, I ended up computerizing everywhere I worked: a mortgage banking company, an invoice processing firm, an automotive plating shop, an insurance agency. Nothing too challenging, until I became the youngest woman among eight in the Taco Bell headquarters accounting department. (Funny how men subjugated women but trusted us to count their money and teach their young.)

I helped automate the franchisees for the first few months but was soon in charge of the entire accounting group. No fun. Gloria, the self-appointed leader who had been there the longest and did the most mind-numbing, repetitive tasks, was old enough to be my mother, and I had been programmed to respect my elders. I soon modified the adage: Respect your elders *if* they are competent.

## MY FIRST MARRIAGE

Louise Erdrich, a Native American writer who won the Pulitzer Prize in 2021 for her novel *The Night Watchman*, summed up the dangers of holding on to the status quo when she said, "Things which do not grow, and change, are dead things."

My first marriage proved her right. I married Phil Salewski when I was nineteen and he was a twenty-one-year-old marine. I had met his younger brother, Jon, when I was in Seattle after my escape from the nuthouse. Jon thought Phil and I would enjoy being pen pals since Phil was deployed to Vietnam and I was alone on the West Coast. We exchanged letters, and when Phil's tour was over, we got married, having only spent a month together during that year.

We were good friends but not a good match. Phil had dropped out of high school to enlist and barely completed his GED, whereas I had skipped grades in high school. Despite our differences, Phil loved me, and I desperately needed to be loved. We had little in common other than playing pinochle with friends. I knew I needed a strong, decisive partner and mistook Phil's stubbornness for decisiveness. In hindsight, he seemed insecure, never sure of what I would say or do. His need to control me taught me lessons that became fundamental to my career success (see chapter 7).

I had several strikes against me from the start. Quitting school to work so my husband could go to college was what women did in those days. In fact, women of my generation were expected to be teachers, secretaries, or stay-at-home moms and housewives. When Phil and I got married, the only advice my mother gave me was that I always had to agree to do anything my husband wanted. Ugh!

Phil didn't like college, and college didn't like him. He studied to become a civil engineer but didn't make the cut. He decided to become a policeman or a long-haul trucker. We moved back to Minnesota to manage one of my father's apartment buildings (free rent), and Phil applied to police departments.

After four years of trying, our first baby girl, Melissa, was born when I was twenty-three. I worked during the day, gave birth to Melissa at 2 a.m., and called in sick the next morning. Couldn't afford to skip a paycheck. Phil had just landed his dream job of being a cop, and we wanted to buy a house.

I *really* tried to be a stay-at-home mom. I cleaned. I sewed. I learned to knit and crochet. I gardened and even canned vegetables. I tried having coffee with the neighbors. None of it worked too well.

Twenty-two months later, I had our second lovely daughter, Shay. Even with two little ones, I couldn't stay busy. I finally talked Phil into letting me work part-time, and that was that: No more stay-at-home mom for me. I rationalized that I was doing my girls a favor by working. With that much energy and drive, I knew I would be an overbearing mother.

My neighbor, whose husband was also a cop and who had two kids, made a lot of money working as a sales rep. I didn't like talking to people back then, but if Kate could do it, so could I. However, I didn't have a college degree, and I had no previous business experience, two little girls, and a paranoid husband; there was no way I would be allowed to travel 40 percent of the time. I got tired of hearing employment recruiters say, "Face it, lady. Your place is at home, taking care of babies. No one will hire you."

*Not so fast, Mr. Recruiter Man. I'm flexible. I'm nimble. And I will find a way.*

My goal was clear: Make money and don't get bored. I knew where I wanted to end up. Obstacles were merely challenges to overcome. Quite frankly, I never thought about gender bias. I knew I was supposed to be married. Check. I did that. Now give me a job.

That was the juncture. My personal and professional lives split apart and took different paths. My personal life was governed by early programming and mired in muck for years. My professional life gave me the ability to stretch out, flex my muscles, climb mountains, and thrive.

## THE "COMPUTER" WHO SOLD COMPUTERS

In 1976, Olivetti was a large supplier of office equipment, including typewriters, adding machines, and word processors. Female secretaries were their main users. The Minneapolis computer systems branch had earned the dishonor of being the worst in the nation when Ron Spychalski was hired as branch manager. Ron decided the quickest way to catapult his branch to the top was to hire a woman, motivate her, and shame the men into beating her in sales. I was the guinea pig he hired, and it took two years for our branch to become number one in the country. These were not all happy days, however. The gorgeous sales secretary initially refused to type my proposals. She was hired to work for men, not a woman. Fortunately, Ron facilitated her "attitude adjustment."

Olivetti's premier system, the A6, had an eight-inch floppy disc unit hung off the side of a modified Selectric typewriter. There was a series of programmable lights across the front of the console. When the red light on the far right lit up, it signaled, "System is dead. Reboot."

Ron initiated a demonstration contest, and the rep who gave the most prospect demos during the month would win a trip to Mexico. Phil and I had never had a vacation, so I organized as many demos as I could. Due to a shortage of systems, I had to do one in the programmers' office. In the middle of the demo, the dreaded red light came on, the programmers started laughing, and my prospect smirked. I turned and looked. The programmers had written FUCK YOU on the plastic covering the red light.

Ron was livid. He and the programming staff had an immediate come-to-Jesus session. The programmers were given a choice: Apologize to me profusely and support my sales efforts or be fired. After all, the income from my sales paid most of their salaries.

Now it was only the other sales reps who hated me. I had a much easier time getting initial sales appointments than the guys. Olivetti's prospects were small businesses, all owned by men. Most were surprised that a woman had the audacity to call and claim she could help them make more money. They were curious to see what this "broad" looked like and usually agreed to an appointment. Why not take a break during the workday and flirt a bit? I learned to walk the line: Appear to be interested. Be knowledgeable. Stay off limits.

Several years later, Ron took over the Minnesota Sperry Univac branch, and I was his first recruit. The systems were more complicated, the sales cycle longer, and the harassment by the male prospects was relentless. Several times I was told, "You either sleep with me or I'm going to buy your competitor's system." I had a pat answer: "As soon as you sign their contract, bend over and shove it up your ass!" One guy appeared on a local news station and made false allegations about me. Another one called the regional manager in Chicago and told a pack of lies. Fortunately, the men in charge only cared about the revenue I generated.

Back then, I didn't realize I was a pioneer. In fact, I didn't want to be number one in a class of morons. (Yeah, I had some attitude problems.) When Sperry Univac asked to do a spotlight story on me, I refused. (So dumb!) From my own myopic perspective, I didn't want to be acknowledged *because* I was female. I wanted to be the best regardless of gender. Being a novelty act wasn't part of my equation. At the time, I didn't realize that being the "wrong" sex was why I got the job in the first place.

Secret sauce: Sell a lot, make the boss look good, and *then* he will have your back.

## TWO FACES OF ME

On the outside, it looked like I had it all. Married, the mother of two lovely, fascinating little girls, and a successful career. The flip side—the inside of me—told a different story. I was a mess. I felt numb and discombobulated. I wanted so badly to be a good mom, but I was too tired. I made myself physically available for my kids from six to nine each evening, but I could barely stay awake. My husband demanded that I be a proper, traditional wife who cooked, cleaned, and took care of his needs and only talked to women. Our girls needed and deserved my attention, but all I wanted to do was sit in a closet with a bag over my head (figuratively speaking).

Colleagues considered me successful, and I was lauded in the business community. But I felt like a personal failure, lonely and hollowed out. My body armor was cinched up tight to keep from being hurt—lizard skin in place.

I grew tired of pretending and plotting how to make Phil think everything was his idea so that we could have or do what I thought was best. When my paycheck exceeded his, our marriage disintegrated. We divorced when Melissa was six and Shay was four. Two weeks after moving out of the house, Phil invited a lady fourteen years younger to move into his apartment. He came over one night so I could teach him to balance a checkbook.

Now my dad felt he was a failure because three of his four daughters were divorced. Only my oldest sister, Kathy, stayed with her first husband.

When Dad died on October 25, 1979, I was devastated. I knew my father loved me, despite having put me at grave risk when I was a teenager. I worked harder to numb my pain and learned to grieve in sound bites.

During the next four years, my gerbil wheel spun faster: Get up early. Drop the kids off at daycare as soon as it opens. Drive thirty minutes to work. Pick up the kids a second before daycare closes. Take food out of the freezer to stick in the oven. Eat. Do dishes. Play with the girls. Put them to bed. Sit down and work for several more hours. Crash into bed. Wake up. Do it again.

The girls and I made tents, did puzzles, played Chutes and Ladders a million times a night, and threw a basketball around the living room. We were living in a lovely neighborhood with a community tennis court and swimming pool. In the summer, I hired a live-in babysitter, Sue O'Neal, to take care of the girls Monday through Friday while I worked. I refused to talk on the phone when I could spend time with my daughters. I had no friends and no time to make any. I seldom dated. I never introduced the girls to any male friends. I wanted Phil to be the only father figure in their lives.

I wrote this note to myself one night, in the middle of this chaos:

It's tough to show love and affection, much less feel it, when I'm so exhausted, exercising like a madwoman every morning to make my body as tired as my mind. Doing 50 million Sudoku puzzles in a row to recalibrate my mind. I need to make more money. The girls need me to be financially independent. Run faster. Do more . . . I really am a computer who sells computers.

## Never Too Late

Casey spent her childhood swimming, surfing, paddling kayaks, and driving boats. By age twelve, she was the preferred captain of the twenty-one-foot family outboard. One day when she was fourteen, she ran into dense fog on the way to Catalina Island (twenty-six miles across the sea). Captain Casey made port by dead reckoning, no problem.

She asked her dad for career advice when she was a senior in college. He suggested she consider flying planes since she was so good at navigating boats. After one flight lesson, Casey was hooked. She began dreaming of being an international pilot for a major airline. The fact that commercial pilots were predominantly male in the early nineties didn't slow her down.

Casey wanted to have adventures and explore remote places while accumulating the required flight hours. Her favorite professor had shared his fascination with Papua New Guinea (PNG), so when she spotted an advertisement for pilots based in the extreme northwest corner of PNG, she applied. Her first job after getting her license was flying a Cessna 206 for a Catholic mission. Soon she was delivering supplies and miscellaneous stuff to remote villages. She was surprised that the "stuff" included live crocodiles used by the natives to make purses and belts. Casey had no fear when landing a tiny plane on an overgrown, barely marked runway or when entire communities ran alongside her plane during landing.

Casey had one huge fear, however. After she was married, the prospect of pausing her career to have kids terrified her. Casey's identity was being a pilot. Who would she be if she was no longer a pilot? Would she ever be good enough to be rehired once her kids were grown? The question "What if I try and fail?" plagued her.

She loved being a mom, but when the time was right, Casey said yes to overcoming her fear. She worked her way up from flying feeder planes to regular commercial domestic flights. At age fifty-six, Casey's dream finally came true. She is now a first officer, flying the Dreamliner (Boeing 787) for a major international airline and having adventures all over the world.

## THE CHALLENGE THAT ALMOST KILLED ME

It's one thing to challenge the status quo in your own culture. It's a whole other ball game doing it in a foreign culture.

In my late fifties, buoyed by my for-profit success, my arrogance almost killed me. I desperately wanted to introduce income-generating opportunities to the disadvantaged Hamar women. After more than forty days sleeping in a tent and eating spaghetti every day while doing a needs analysis survey, I concluded that the area had only two available resources: acacia thorns and goats. Lots and lots of both.

It really bothered me that the women, who did all the work, were seldom allowed to eat goat. Goat was for the men and boys. Women ate nuts and sorghum. Not fair.

I figured if I gave the men an incentive to kill more goats, perhaps women would get some of the meat. The men wanted money. Goatskin belts required dead goats. I gambled that there would be a market for goatskin belts. My favorite women's cooperative made five trial goatskin belts, which were four double-sided rectangles sewn together with sinew. The women decorated the belts with cheap beads and cowrie shells. I was delighted and took them back to America with me and sold them to supporters. The belts looked weird and weren't comfortable, but I still thought we might be able to sell a few more.

When I returned to the area a few months later, hundreds of Hamar women greeted me with more than 2,000 goatskin belts. I was appalled. The belts looked awful, the women looked gleeful, and I felt terrified. I didn't have close to enough money in my backpack to pay for the belts. (Only "legal" entities are allowed to have a bank account in Ethiopia, and I was not legal at that time.) Hamar men were sitting on the ground, their AK-47s resting on their shoulders, waiting for me to pay.

I wanted to cry, jump in the Land Cruiser, and run away. Instead, I convinced them that I only had money to pay for 500 of them, and in the morning, I would suggest how the remaining 1,500 belts could be revised into different products that I would buy on my next trip.

During that long, tortuous night, the only things I could think of making out of the rectangles were bookmarks, dog chews, napkin rings, and Christmas tree ornaments. Try explaining bookmarks to someone who has never seen a book and then tackle Christmas tree ornaments and napkin rings. Each of the belts had eight rectangles of goat skin. Each ornament, bookmark, dog chew, and napkin ring used one rectangle. My duffel bags were full of 12,000 marginal doodads for the next trip out. I think we ended up selling about 25 goatskin belts and 500 doodads. The dog chews were the most popular. At least I got out of there alive.

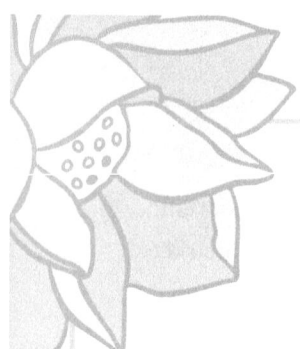

# DREAM:
## Challenging the Status Quo

**D**esire: Have the creativity to think, *What if?* and the courage to respond, *Why not me?*

**R**eflect on what I want to make, do, or become that is contrary to social norms.

**E**xplore barriers that need to crumble to improve my (or others') experience.

**A**cknowledge that there will be times when I feel unwelcome and full of doubt.

**M**antra:
I will not compromise who I am,
What I know to be true.
I will not conform to belong.

### WISE WOMAN WORDS

"Any woman who chooses to behave like a full human being
Should be warned that the armies of the status quo
Will treat her as something of a dirty joke.
That's their natural and first weapon.
She will need her sisterhood."
—*Gloria Steinem*

# 6

# Understanding the Power of WIIFM

What's in it for me? That's the essence of WIIFM. Saying yes to its power means striving to understand the needs of others so we can use vocabulary and context they understand *and are able to process.*

The "me" can be the person we are trying to convince or the person we fear. "Me" might be someone trying to help us or an adversary determined to undermine us. Perhaps the "me" is a group of people who live in an environment so different from ours that they cannot fathom what we are talking about.

No matter the situation, at home or in a place far from your comfort zone, strive to stand in "me's" shoes to identify what benefits that person or what those people need or want to accomplish. For example, what will make "me" feel important or safe, provide the benefits "me" wants, or help "me" reach their goal?

### WIIFM WORKS

On my first day as Olivetti's first female computer sales rep, the regional product sales manager was waiting for me. I was informed that after he trained me for two days, I would be on my own, selling the Olivetti A5 to pharmacies to manage prescriptions. In 1976, most drugstores were small businesses owned by the pharmacist; prescription labels were hand-typed, and without integrated systems, it was nearly impossible to check for drug incompatibilities.

The Olivetti solution sounded ideal. When the prescription was typed into the A5, the label would print, a record of the prescription was stored on a dollar-bill-size magnetic-striped card for easy refills, and a summary of the prescription was automatically typed on a patient profile ledger card that could be quickly reviewed for drug incompatibilities. The ledger cards were specially designed with a pocket to store all the prescription mag cards.

The WIIFM for the hardworking pharmacist was easy: saving time with automatic printing of labels for refills and an innovative patient profile.

The big gotcha, however, was that a typical pharmacy managed over 10,000 prescriptions and had approximately 5,000 customers. Each prescription required one mag card, and each customer needed a ledger card envelope. Sales were great the first year, but they quickly slowed down once word spread that the drugstores using the Olivetti A5 program no longer had sufficient room for retail merchandise. Their storage space was overrun with magnetic-striped and ledger cards. Despite these challenges, I sold a lot of A5 computers.

My first customer suffered a nervous breakdown nine months after the sale, and I've always wondered if his A5 purchase had anything to do with it. I had nightmares for weeks, picturing a tornado of mag cards swirling around me while I tossed and turned, trying to sleep.

### SWIRLING CHAOS

Single mom with two little girls, thirty years old, drowning in mag cards—something other than the ground had to shift. Time to change a variable. My Olivetti boss, Ron, took over the Sherry Univac branch and hired me to sell manufacturing application systems. I loved the complexities of the market and quickly excelled. My innate love for efficiency and productivity had found the perfect lucrative outlet.

Even though I was one of 3 women and more than 700 men who made their annual quota, by 1982 I realized that I'd never make it to the top at Sperry Univac. I was the wrong gender, and I didn't have a college degree. It was time for me to move on, so I quit my job with its reliable paycheck and leaped into the great unknown. In all honesty, I don't think this decision qualifies as an example of the magic of yes, as it was more like "What the heck are you doing when you have two children to support?"

### Changes at Warp Speed

Today, most of us go about our daily lives phone in hand, with the ability to communicate with just about anyone and access the world's knowledge bases at whim. That certainly was not the case in the seventies and eighties. During those years, my career spanned multiple generations of computing—from service bureaus to timeshares to automated bookkeeping machines, punch cards, and mag cards; from hard discs to eight-inch floppy discs to three-and-a-half-inch diskettes providing storage for 4K microcomputers. Software for personal computers transitioned from recipe-box replacements to productivity software (spreadsheets, databases, and word processing) to complex business applications—all in less than five years.

The phrase "World Wide Web" (www) was first discussed for business in the late eighties. The role of the computer sales rep also changed from being a highly technical one-on-one expert to being a computer store clerk, then to telesales and on to today's world of no one physically being there. Download the app, cross your fingers, and click.

## LUCKY, LUCKY ME

An unexpected parachute appeared during my jump into the unknown. One of my prospects had developed a shop data collection system and hired me to bring it to market. My projected confidence in my ability to figure out what needed to be done hid a lack of proven marketing expertise. I was lucky, though, and my first consulting gig ended up being magical—not because of the product (it was a dud) but because my client provided me with access to the major players of the budding microcomputer industry.

A small, intimate computer forum was orchestrated by a venture capital group exploring the viability of microcomputer technology. Young, brilliant entrepreneurs and intrapreneurs (Bill Gates of Microsoft, Steve Jobs of Apple, Bob Roach of Radio Shack, Phil Estridge of IBM, Adam Osborne of Osborne Computers, etc.) were assembled to convince potential investors of four key things:

1. They knew what they were doing.
2. Their technology was durable.
3. Their company or division would survive.
4. Their start-up was the best investment opportunity.

There were only 100 people at this amazing event, and I was one of them!

A few months later, I attended a conference in Dallas, Texas, where I heard people position themselves as experts able to predict the future of microcomputing. I remember thinking, *What makes them an expert? I can feel the market exploding. Why don't I go back to Minnesota and declare myself an expert?* So, that's what I did. I became a self-declared expert on microcomputers and started my software company, JobBOSS Software. I was a single mom with two young girls, $1,000 in my savings account, and no clue about the challenges and pitfalls ahead of me.

While selling manufacturing systems to larger companies for Sperry Univac, I discovered that job shops (made-to-order manufacturers who fabricated, machined, or molded metal) desperately needed software to manage their workload. Their requirements sounded the same as the big guys' but were fundamentally different. The big guys made their millions by controlling material costs, while the little guys made their slim profits by controlling labor costs.

Different needs require different systems.

By understanding the job shop's needs and feeling their pain, we were able to design the best product for their pocketbook. Our software organized, analyzed, processed, and leveraged the thousands of details that convert metal and plastic into usable parts. The only problem was I had no money, and tiny JobBOSS was on the leading (bleeding) edge of integrating software for microcomputers.

## HIGH-PRICE BAILOUT

David was born when Shay was eight and Melissa was ten. Nowadays, having sex out of wedlock is no big deal for most people, and I'm sure my daughters couldn't care less, but back then, the taboos were fierce, and I bought into that crap. Talk about programming.

The idea of managing three kids as a single mom—financially, psychologically, and physically—scared me. I'd spent so many years focused on my work that I became devastated, knowing I was a bad role model for my girls. Something had to give, and back then I was still susceptible to peer pressure about the status quo.

Besides feeling social pressure, I was broke. We were living hand to mouth. I was in a panic and had no idea how to support my children. And then I met Steve, who was available: single, socially acceptable, and, best of all, willing to accept me with three kids. He graciously made the last few house payments before we got married. I was grateful that I could keep working. My work defined me. If I had chosen a mantra at the time (which is laughable), it might've been something like "Personal heartache, professional pride." Sad but true.

Once again, the darn early programming I had been subjected to was determining my behavior. Being single was wanton and sinful. Marriage was the right thing to do, and it was encouraged and required.

Steve was a traveling zipper salesman. We had fun before we got married, but everything changed after the "big day." Instead of remaining spontaneous and carefree, he became strict and controlling. This was particularly tough on Melissa. She and Steve butted heads, and she always lost. I was torn asunder (old-fashioned word, but that's how it felt: ripped in half) between the supposed-to wife role and the compassionate mom. Unfortunately, I was too tired and emotionally exhausted to argue Melissa's case. She hated Steve and rightly so.

To make matters worse, shortly after we were married, Steve announced that he had worked long enough, and he wanted to stay home. Be Mr. Mom. He wanted to cook, clean (uh, supervise Melissa and Shay doing the cleaning), and watch David.

Sounded good. I could work more. Really bad decision. Steve hated Melissa and liked Shay and David—as long as they did what he said. I started thinking about divorcing him on our wedding day. I rationalized staying in the relationship because even though it was not good for Melissa, I thought it was good for Shay and David, and, of course, I could keep working. It took me twenty-five years to finally say, "Enough."

## REFUGE IN WORK

I felt comfortable and competent with job shop owners. We were all entrepreneurs. I understood the heartache and frustration of being underfunded and overworked and having confidence in a dream that at times was based only on intuition and a belief that we had created something special.

I often think that we entrepreneurs are "missing a chip." We just don't know how to be afraid of the unknown. I did know the power of WIIFM, however. Living with Phil had taught me well, and WIIFM was going to be my secret sauce.

As JobBOSS grew, we made sure that everyone on our team could relate to job shop owners. Everyone learned the terms used on the shop floor so they would sound credible. A key element of new-employee orientation was touring customer shops and meeting folk, from receptionists to programmers to salespeople to key decision-makers, so they would understand the totality of the shop environment. Everyone in the organization was given the chance to stand in the shop manager's and shop employees' shoes. Not only did these activities help JobBOSS employees make an emotional connection with our customers, but it also fueled team spirit within our company.

Using WIIFM helps build a bridge from your current environment to your goal. It can make other people's jobs easier and more efficient. It makes meetings more relevant. Understanding what other people care about—their perspective, what matters to them, their environment, their fears, and their concerns—gives you the ability to persuade, to influence, and to make a positive difference.

## PERSUASION POWER

In a 1998 article in *Harvard Business Review* titled "The Necessary Art of Persuasion," Jay Conger, an organizational behavior professor, states that persuasion is not about convincing or selling.[16] It's about learning and negotiating.

Persuasion requires four critical elements:

- *Credibility* is usually based on expertise. You are perceived as knowledgeable in, and experienced with, a particular subject. The other basis for building credibility is through relationships. You have demonstrated a genuine interest in and commitment to what matters to the other party.

---

16    Jay Conger, "The Necessary Art of Persuasion," *Harvard Business Review*, May–June 1998.

- *Common ground* is needed to gain perspective. Seek to understand what specifically interests the other party, why, and how they currently satisfy that interest. Open a dialogue about the issue and listen to *their* ideas and concerns.
- *Vivid evidence* is necessary, too. Don't expect someone to take your word. That said, factual data and reams of spreadsheets and charts are not highly persuasive. People respond to "evidence" that brings your concept or argument to life. Experiential proof, such as metaphors, analogies that make your ideas tangible, and stories of direct experiences, causes shifts in people's perspectives and allows them to "see" the situation through the eyes of others who support what you are doing. It allows them to experience WIIFM.
- *Emotional connections* establish that you are plugged into another person's needs. Emotions are primary factors in motivation and decision-making. They help facilitate a shared understanding of the issue and what is at stake. Sense the emotions of the other person and try to mirror your tone and intensity to fit theirs, whether it means showing enthusiasm and passion or anger and frustration.

## MOTIVATING WIIFM

A key resource that provides the power and volition to help us reach our goals is other people who need to be motivated. As individuals, we respond to different stimuli and feel valued in different ways. Some of us strive for recognition. Some of us want to feel needed. Others are motivated by money, and many people want to feel like they make a difference. An individual's driving force is their WIIFM, the fuel that propels them forward.

Another tactic to understanding WIIFM is to identify the other person's personality type so we can establish an emotional connection by adjusting our vocabulary and pace to theirs. At JobBOSS, we used the Wilson Learning Center model, which divides social styles (personality types) into four categories:

- *Drivers* like to cut to the chase. They are forceful and quick to make decisions. They may need you to get right to the point or focus a little more on the problem at hand and less on the people involved.
- *Analyticals* rely on a structured approach and facts. They like data and often need time to double-check your evidence and think things through. They want to be sure of the information.
- *Expressives* are enthusiastic and want to hear excitement in your voice. They want flexibility and tend to be spontaneous. They like an enthusiastic collaboration and buy-in.
- *Amiables* want you to be open and honest about your feelings. They don't want to feel hurried. They tend to rely on the support of others and like an interactive approach to problem-solving.

Since about 25 percent of people fall into each of these four categories, you share a social style with only about 25 percent of the people you meet. To use the power of WIIFM with the other 75 percent, you need to be versatile.

JobBOSS, a typical software company, had four disparate teams of employees, each with a preferred way of receiving and processing information. Programmers, accounting, and administrative personnel tended to be analytical. They needed a detailed, logical sequence to what was being requested. Customer service people were analytical but were also amiable, with the ability to make a quick emotional connection with the client. Salespeople were expressive, often described as "people people." At times, though, they liked to cut corners.

We used the Myers–Briggs test internally to help our teams reduce their frustration with each other and to encourage the analytical processors (programmers) to appreciate the strengths of the enthusiastic expressives (salespeople), who kept promising the impossible when it came to product enhancements. Having everyone take the Myers–Briggs and participate in exercises to understand the behavioral traits of others made a difference. It improved communication and joint problem-solving and reduced the eye rolls and muttering between the teams.

## RISING ABOVE THE FRAY

The power of WIIFM is not limited to interpersonal communication. It can also be used by underfunded companies with no money for advertising and to overcome flyover-state syndrome.

In the late eighties, the microcomputer industry was a messy hodgepodge. Prior to Microsoft and Apple emerging as dominant players, zillions of little companies were scrambling to tout their widget or gadget as the one that would tie everything together. Printers did not talk to computers; internet connectivity was slow and painful; networks crashed regularly; and suppliers were here today and gone tomorrow.

On top of that, JobBOSS was in Minnesota, a flyover state between Silicon Valley and Boston. Programmers were in such high demand that new computer science graduates with no experience were demanding $50,000-per-year salaries, double the starting salaries for other positions. We couldn't compete when it came to money, so we needed to find an alternative approach. Enter *Inc.* magazine.

*Inc.* magazine delivers advice, tools, and services to help small business owners and CEOs grow their companies more successfully. Most importantly, it started to publish the *Inc.* 500 list of the 500 fastest-growing independent, privately held corporations, proprietorships, or partnerships. To be eligible, a company had to show a sales history of at least five years, with sales year number one exceeding $50,000. I figured our best chance to make the list was in 1991, when our compound five-year growth rate would be calculated using the lowest possible denominator. We made our goal! We were number 334 on the 1991 list and were invited to the annual *Inc.* conference at no charge.

To make the most of this opportunity, we needed free publicity, which meant getting *Inc.* to publish stories about us. JobBOSS needed to be positioned as the perfect example for an article that an *Inc.* writer thought would entice the editor to publish. My three days at the conference were spent chatting up various writers and trying to sniff out storylines.

The strategy paid huge dividends. One writer liked the idea of being a silent witness when six of my employees, one from each team, conducted a "peer" employee review of me, the CEO/founder. The writer flew in, the review was conducted, and a story appeared in the next issue of *Inc.*, discussing the innovative approach. Nothing like putting oneself out there.

After that, JobBOSS became the darling of *Inc.* magazine. Several years later, *Inc.* ran a contest for the "Best Small Company to Work for in the USA," and we were one of the winners, based on employee participation and empowerment. This award helped us hire the best employees available for modest salaries. We became recognized as a model company for participatory management, thanks to the power of WIIFM.

## WIIFM DOESN'T ALWAYS TRANSLATE

Seeking to understand others can be a steep mountain to climb, depending on your environment. It often requires patience and endurance. Imagine that your native language (Hamar) is only an oral language and has less than 1,000 words, none of which describe a concept, idea, or unknown. Only one word is used for everything good, and one word indicates all forms of bad. There are only words for nouns and action verbs. There are none for feelings, needs, or concerns or to describe ideas. All time is kept by the position of the sun and the moon, and days are tracked by blades of grass tied into knots.

Now imagine learning a second language (Amharic), a syllabary (not an alphabet) of around 500 combinations of seven vowels and thirty-one consonants. To further complicate matters, the questions you have been paid to ask were developed in an advanced language (English) filled with homonyms, synonyms, and antonyms.

How do you learn and understand new words for which you have no basis? How do you map the new words to your original vocabulary?

My first goal in South Omo Valley, Ethiopia, was to understand what the Hamar tribe needed for a chance at a healthy life. From the jump, we had vocabulary problems. For example, what does "healthy" mean? How do you know what "bad" feels like if you've never experienced "good"? What does "experience" mean?

I spent forty days trying to understand Hamar's WIIFM. My team and I soon limited ourselves to asking three questions to three people per day. It was exhausting and hot and a real lesson in patience for me.

Lori speaking to Hamar elder: "Help me understand what will make you feel better."

Amharic translator to Hamar translator: (Several Amharic speakers discuss this for fifteen minutes before relaying words to Hamar translator.)

Hamar translator to elder: (Several words taking less than one minute.)

Elder to Hamar translator: (Ten words or less.)

Hamar translator to Amharic translator: (Discussion among themselves for ten minutes.)

Amharic translator to Lori: "He wants you to bring him some beer."

Lori to Amharic translator: "Please tell me what you asked him."

Amharic translator to Lori: "I asked him what you wanted me to ask him."

Lori to Amharic translator: "Please review with me your understanding of my question."

Amharic translator to Lori: "Give me my money. I quit!"

Eventually, things simplified, and we found translators who were able to understand what I was trying to identify. I also learned enough Hamar words to know when the translator was talking about the weather versus asking my question. After interviewing more than 100 people, including elders, women, teachers, government workers, and teenagers, we finally identified their WIIFM.

The Hamar are an ancient tribe who have survived for years by following in the footsteps of their ancestors. By the time I met them in 2008, the elders knew this was no longer sufficient.

"Our ancestors prospered," they kept saying, "but when we do as they did, we barely survive. What are we doing wrong?"

These wise men were at a loss because their environment (social, economic, ecological) had changed, and no one had helped them build the necessary bridges to adapt. They begged for "new awareness" so they could help themselves. They wanted to know what they didn't know.

Somehow, we needed to determine what had to change for them to have a chance for a healthy life. Not only would they need expensive new inputs (water, schools, income-generating activities), but they would also have to change centuries-old behaviors to take advantage of and sustain these new assets.

Using the power of WIIFM made it possible for our programs to be wildly successful. We were able to look at issues through Indigenous African eyes. Analyzing needs and creating strategies to motivate people to change traditional behavior required out-of-the-box thinking. Wait until you read about encouraging the Hamar tribal members to practice family planning and use pit latrines.

## KOLE KILKALA: THE ENLIGHTENED WARRIOR

In a previous chapter, we discussed how we don't need to be educated or have social or economic advantages to become successful entrepreneurs. Leonardo da Vinci exemplifies what someone can accomplish with insatiable curiosity and perseverance.

In South Omo Valley, I met another wonderful example of this: Kole Kilkala. Kole is the owner of the Keske campsite perched on the banks of the mighty Keske river. Mighty, that is, when there is a flash flood caused by heavy rains in the highlands, hundreds of miles away. Usually, the Keske is just a sandy riverbed. Kole is remarkable. He is a clear thinker and understands his community's responsibility for change. He is hungry for more information. A real outlier.

Less than ten years before I met him, Kole was a simple, uneducated pastoralist who happened to own property next to the Keske well and dry riverbed. One day, a tourist set up camp next to the riverbed and spent the day sitting under one of Kole's trees. When the tourist packed up his tent and left, he gave Kole five birr (about fifty-five cents). Several months later, another tourist camped in the same place, sat under Kole's trees, and gave him ten birr when he left. Kole decided he had something of value and started telling tour companies in the area that he had a campsite for them. For fifteen birr per night per tent, Kole would let them camp there, and he provided toilets (a tin shed with a hole in the ground) and showers (tin sheds with an elevated plastic container that was filled with water and had a hole in it plugged by a nail).

He has constantly improved the place. Kole and I made a deal that every time I stopped in, he would give me a warm bottle of Coke, and I would help him think of new ways to improve his campsite to make more money. Keske Campsite is generally sold out, and Kole is now a well-respected elder of the community.

## Flexibility Is Key

Marge had a master plan. She and her husband, Al, agreed that when their youngest son, Bobby, started middle school, she would work part-time for the most successful flower shop in the area and discover the secret to their success. Then, in three years, when Bobby started high school, she would be ready to run a shop of her own.

Marge pounced when the owner of a mediocre

flower shop five miles away decided to sell. She was ready for action. On day one, she rolled out a special promo package for mortuaries and local churches within a ten-mile radius. Her goal was to become the florist of choice for funerals, weddings, and special events. Although Marge and Al were not churchgoers, they forced Bobby to attend Sunday School, hoping to win points with the church people. Marge volunteered to chair the local chamber of commerce welcome committee. Suddenly, members received incentives to send flowers (discounted at Marge's shop) to new businesses opening in the community. What? A nail salon receiving flowers from a tire shop?

Business blossomed (couldn't pass up the pun) until Bobby got a job on a fishing boat and their older daughter moved to Oregon to teach school. Marge's cheap labor disappeared, and she had no experience being a "real" employer. She knew how to coerce family members to work ridiculous hours during crunch time, but team building, employee recognition, and merit pay? What was that all about?

The next few years were chaotic, with constant employee turnover, sleepless nights, and new blood pressure meds. Eventually, desperation buried Marge's pride, and she signed up for a human resource class at the community college. Once she admitted she needed help, she tackled learning with a vengeance. She wanted to understand why employees were quitting. Her instructor explained that an employee satisfaction survey could identify each person's key motivating factor. It surprised her to learn that employees wanted more freedom in floral designs and yearned to be recognized for a job well done. Marge was relieved to discover what they wanted were variables she could control and didn't cost more money.

## WIIFM CAN CHANGE POLICY

Saying yes to the power of WIIFM can help us as individuals, and it has also influenced military tactics and altered the course of a country.

This story, shared by the district commander of the Coast Guard, Rear Admiral Gary Blore, recounts how the military used WIIFM to save the lives of Native American fishermen in Alaska.

To reduce the number of fishermen drowning, the Coast Guard issued 1,000 orange life jackets. The fishermen refused to wear them, claiming that the orange would attract polar bears. Even though the Coast Guard provided the elders with reams of information showing that not to be true, the elders refused. After four months of deliberation, the Coast Guard had 1,000 white life jackets made. The fishermen wear them eagerly. True, the white vest is much harder for the Coast Guard to see amid the ice, but more men live because they are wearing life jackets. Understanding the WIIFM of the fishermen helped the Coast Guard switch from improving their metrics on the number of rescues to focusing on the number of lives saved.

More than 150 years ago, Ethiopia was prosperous. The land was fertile, and the people worked hard. According to folklore, Egypt was jealous and fearful of Ethiopia's expanding influence due to its growing economy. The grand Orthodox patriarch, an Egyptian, was quite strategic and set out to undermine Ethiopia's prosperity. He decided to radically increase the number of religious holidays to forty-five days per year and require the Ethiopian Orthodox to worship on those days. Work was forbidden. The drastically reduced number of workdays damaged Ethiopia's productivity, the economy slowed down, and now it is one of the poorest countries in the world. I can't confirm the veracity of this story, but it's a fascinating effort to justify the decline.

WIIFM has played an important part in helping me say no and set boundaries; understanding why people (including myself) behave as they do paves the way to forgiveness and moving on. The use of

WIIFM has removed roadblocks and allowed me to successfully challenge the status quo. Tuning in to the emotions of another person and understanding their perspective has made it easier to build a bridge from my starting point to my desired goal.

# D R E A M:
## *Understanding the Power of WIIFM*

**D**esire: Expand my understanding of situations by appreciating and integrating different perspectives.

**R**eflect on what would concern me if I were the other person.

**E**xplore the core issues with an open mind prior to responding.

**A**cknowledge that I need to actively listen and seek to understand.

**M**antra:
Let me walk in your shoes, breathe the air you breathe,
Smell the fragrances of your life so I may understand your needs.

### WISE WOMAN WORDS

"People may not remember exactly what you did, or what you said, but they will always remember how you made them feel."
—Maya Angelou

# 7

# Taking Risks to Embrace New Opportunities

Soon after we are born, we begin taking risks and trying new things. A baby takes her first step and then falls. We stand her up, and she takes two more steps and falls once more. Over and over, again and again. Whether learning to ride a bike, kick a soccer ball, or kiss someone new without bumping noses, we learn by taking risks and embracing opportunities.

When did we stop? Why? What happened to us?

Perhaps your parents were overprotective and controlled your environment or you were shamed for failing to perform simple tasks. Maybe your personality is inherently more cautious or your culture emphasizes conformity. No matter what the reason, in order to grow and evolve, you need to start over by reverting to the "original you."

How? Baby steps. Fall. Get up. Step again. Rinse and repeat. First a small risk, then bigger, until you reach the top of the hill and see a new, compelling view of the world. Now instead of being a gerbil running faster and faster and doing the same thing over and over on an endless wheel, you become a circus performer on a flying trapeze (with a safety net below, just in case). You grow. New options appear, providing new paths to explore. New ideas present new opportunities. You're motivated. Energized. Your engine purrs with a full tank of gas.

## FACING FEAR

We all know that lurking beneath every risk is an element of uncertainty and fear—a fear of failure, to be exact; so let's talk about it.

According to mental health writer Lisa Fritscher in "The Psychology of Fear," fear is likely evolutionary and a crucial survival mechanism.[17] It is both a primal, automatic emotion and a highly individual emotional response. Fear produces a biochemical reaction that alerts us to the presence of physical or psychological danger or the threat of harm. The body's physical response is often called the fight-or-flight response—when our bodies prepare to either enter combat or run away. Sometimes fear stems from real threats, but it can also originate from imagined dangers and lead to distress and disruption when it's extreme or out of proportion to the actual threat.

I believe there is a third, healthier alternative to fight-or-flight that can be learned from the animal kingdom.

I once saw an antelope that was being chased by a lion collapse and play dead. Instead of breaking stride and pouncing on the inert antelope, the lion lunged past it in pursuit of another antelope still in motion. The first antelope shakily stood up, shook off her fear, and scampered away. We can do something similar in a scary situation.

Fear is bottled-up adrenaline. We can duck or take a time-out, wait for our heartbeat to slow down and our breathing to return to normal. Or we can learn to harness this energy and roll it into a powerful ball of forward momentum. We can learn to convert our fear into positive energy and action. Probably not the first time we try or even the second, but eventually, we *can* learn to do this.

Fear improves concentration and focuses the mind. People often focus on the threat instead of the solution, but it is possible to train yourself to let fear help you recognize roadblocks, hurdles, or

---

17   Lisa Fritscher, "The Psychology of Fear," Verywellmind, updated April 20, 2024, https://www.verywellmind.com/the-psychology-of-fear-2671696.

bottlenecks. We can use the flip side of our fear to help us build a better bridge to reach our goal.

Lyn Christian, coach, consultant, TEDx speaker, author, and founder of the business coaching company SoulSalt Inc., says, "The psychology of safety teaches us that as individuals, we naturally analyze tasks as they relate to our physical, emotional, and mental well-being. If we think that carrying out a certain action will put us at risk of danger or failure, we tend to avoid this to protect ourselves. . . . But this state of mind can also limit our true potential and erect a barrier to creating the life we want to live."[18]

In my experience, something magical happens when we challenge ourselves and take chances. Science backs this up and posits that risky thinking opens us to challenging situations, which lead to lessons learned, inching us closer to success.

Consider the words of the iconic playwright Neil Simon: "If no one ever took risks, Michelangelo would have painted the Sistine floor."

### RISK AND REWARD

Sometimes, a foolhardy risk pays dividends. The American Institute of Banking agreed to pay me $1,000 per day to teach bank presidents once people started applying for loans to purchase personal computers. I taught classes in word processing, spreadsheets, and database management. My body paid the price, however, since I was six months into an unplanned pregnancy and had to schlep heavy desktop computers.

The moment the daycare door was unlocked, my sleepy little girls were ushered inside. I would race downtown. Double-park, waddle my way through five trips, grunting and groaning, hauling desktop computers into the building to stack them in front of the elevator,

---

18  Lyn Christian, "Taking a Risk in Life: 5-Steps for Determining Worthwhile Risks and Achieving Your Goals," SoulSalt, October 12, 2020, https://soulsalt.com/taking-a-risk-in-life/.

praying they would not be damaged or stolen. I'd then waddle as quickly as I could to my car and search for a parking spot. Fifteen minutes later, reenter the office building, drag the computers into the elevator, trying to catch my breath while it whirred to floor 3, then haul them out and into the training room. I was exhausted before I started my full day of teaching on my feet.

It never occurred to me to ask for help or to hire a helper. I ignored the pain screaming in my gut and back. When the class was over, I had to drag all the computers back to the elevator and reverse the agonizing process. "Lumbering Lori" I called myself. I went home, made dinner for my two little girls, played with them until bedtime, crashed, got up, and repeated the process the next day. Even though I abused my body while pregnant, I gave birth to my perfect little boy with no harm done to him, thankfully.

When I was eight months pregnant with no guaranteed income, I hired my first employee, Henry. Talk about having blind faith in my ability to make money if I just worked harder! I realized that I would never be able to support my family by just consulting. I had to have a "kerchunka machine," a product that could make money while I slept. Henry was tasked with writing the first version of the JobBOSS software program.

Three weeks after giving birth, I decided that to sell my yet-to-be-developed software, we needed a booth at a trade show. My friend Percy brilliantly designed three big panels depicting the most common fears of buying computers at that time. One panel depicted a scared little man quaking in front of a huge, looming computer and another a big hen dwarfing a little guy, accusing him of being "chicken." The third panel was an illustration of an old monstrosity of a computer in mothballs. The three major fears of that time: fear of the unknown, fear of using a computer, and fear of buying something soon to be out-of-date. Eye-catching and radical. Fear sells! It can also be a great motivator.

Shortly after Steve and I were married, I started using his paycheck to pay Henry, my employee. As soon as Steve discovered what I was doing, he put a stop to it and forced me to get a job with a paycheck. Luck intervened when I convinced another struggling company, DigiGraphics, to assume my fledgling company's debt, hire my programmer, and allow him to continue to work on our job shop program. In return, I promised to increase the sales of DigiGraphics' manufacturing software products.

Long story short, unbeknownst to me, DigiGraphics was teetering on the edge of bankruptcy, and after five months of receiving a paycheck, I repossessed my rudimentary job shop program, still saddled with debt. I left DigiGraphics with even more liability—an executive with a pedigree I thought would attract funding who wanted to be a CEO, a marketing person, systems analyst, admin person, and two programmers. By this time, JobBOSS had a handful of customers and a three-year office lease with six months of "free" rent.

## BEING BRAVE WITHOUT BRAVADO

Unfortunately, the free rent ran out, and we missed one month's payroll. Steve was furious. One day, at coffee (who has time to go out for coffee when they're working?), he met a guy, Paul Pettinger, who had a partner, Jack Crowther, who needed someone to run one of his small software companies, which was having difficulty navigating shaky markets. A meeting was quickly arranged, and Jack and I hit it off. Intrigued, Jack sent Paul to visit our office as part of his due diligence. Things got dicey when Paul was greeted by the Do Not Enter sheriff's tape crisscrossing our office doorway. We hadn't paid rent for month seven and had been evicted.

The timing really sucked. I had finally met a man who was willing to invest in JobBOSS the day our office was shut down. The next day, our little company was physically divided between the laundry room in my house and Henry's basement. Our wannabe CEO, marketing lady, and admin people left to find paychecks elsewhere. Four of us (two programmers, a systems analyst, and me) decided to risk it for a few more months. Jack had second thoughts.

I swear you could taste the tension in our house. Negative energy engulfed us like a thick, heavy fog. Everyone was miserable. Steve stomped around, furious at me. The girls hid in their rooms, trying to stay out of sight. My scurrying around, trying to placate everyone, made matters worse. Only David seemed to thrive. He was such a happy, content little guy.

I don't know how we survived those months. It was an emotionally damaging time for all of us. I promised Steve that I would have a job that paid actual money by April 15, 1985. My backup plan was to drive a school bus. I called Jack repeatedly and made more promises. Just when I was ready to start sending my résumé to school districts, Jack decided I was worth the risk, invested $25,000, and guaranteed a desperately needed bank line of credit.

Getting the office stuff out of the laundry room and finally receiving a paycheck helped ease the tension between Steve and me, but not much else improved. The girls were starting middle school and needed my emotional support. David was back in childcare. JobBOSS was gobbling up my energy, and Steve demanded I spend more time with him.

I felt like that middle-age sandwich with everyone taking bites out of me. I knew that my insatiable drive to achieve was making my family miserable, but I didn't know how to fix it. I was convinced I would implode as a stay-at-home mom. I was responsible for three kids. Steve wanted to quit work and be Mr. Mom. And I had a dream, named JobBOSS.

Run! Run! Spin the gerbil wheel faster.

## LOANS WITH NO COLLATERAL

Even with Jack's investment, growing JobBOSS was a dicey venture. Our tiny office was in Minneapolis, Minnesota, and job shops were concentrated near the manufacturing hubs of Detroit, Chicago, Cincinnati, Los Angeles, and the Northeast. Our budget could only be stretched for travel if we were sure to pick up multiple orders per trip.

Want to survive? Take risks.

Out-of-town job shop owners wanted to see the actual program operate before they committed to purchasing it, which was a reasonable demand, but since they didn't own a computer, it wasn't practical for us to send them a demo diskette. Besides, most shop owners had never used a computer.

We experimented. First, we tried working with the hundreds of franchised computer stores that suddenly appeared. That strategy didn't work because the software took too much expertise to sell. Next, we hired remote sales reps, one for Chicago and one for Cincinnati. That didn't work because we didn't have a sales training/support organization. The salesperson needed to be credible, make an emotional connection with the prospect, and provide vivid evidence. They needed to be expert shop management advisors. We could motivate and adequately train salespeople in Minneapolis but not remotely. We had to find a way for our local team to conduct the survey, give the demo, and close the deal a thousand miles away. These were the "olden days," when the ability to instantly download software to your telephone wasn't even a dream.

Aha! There *was* a way. Every shop had fax machines plugged into a dedicated phone line. It was their technology connection to customers and vendors. And Compaq had just introduced their portable computer—the size of a large, heavy shoebox—that could run our program. We purchased several Compaq computers and started shipping them out to prospects "on loan." The Minnesota sales rep became adept at conducting the survey over the phone and convincing the prospect to unplug his precious fax machine and plug in our loaner computer, which was preloaded with *his* sample data. The sales rep would walk the prospect through the pertinent functions. By the end of the demo, the prospect was hooked on the product *and* felt confident in his ability to operate the system. Sale made. During this two-year program, those rugged Compaq portables crisscrossed the country more than 200 times. We never lost a computer.

## (B)LEADING EDGE

MS-DOS was the business microcomputer operating system of the eighties. Soon, however, the buzz of user-friendly, intuitive Windows was everywhere, touted as the future of computing. JobBOSS had been profitable in its first five years, and I was arrogant. I made the decision to rewrite our software for the Windows operating system two years too early. We lost over $1,000,000, and our bank canceled our credit line. I was guilty of taking a risk that was a blind gamble. I did not take the time to understand the complexities or the consequences of the risk.

Bravado, not bravery.

I wanted to be first to market, so "Katie, bar the door." That decision hurt JobBOSS financially, and we lost some wonderful team members. Demotivated and discouraged, it took several years to regroup, reestablish our line of credit, and become profitable again.

## WHERE'S THE EXIT?

I started JobBOSS when David was an infant, Shay was eight, and Melissa ten. For the next fifteen years, JobBOSS consumed most of my energy. Steve kept harping that my free time had to be spent with him. Same old story. I was numb, burned out, not equipped to be the wife Steve wanted nor the mom my kids needed and deserved. It was time to sell the business.

How do you find a buyer of a small company in an "unsexy" small market niche without scaring off potential customers and demotivating employees? I had finally learned my lesson and took time to plan.

My board of directors and I examined the complexities of raising the profile of JobBOSS among the venture capital and investment banking community without negatively impacting the current business. We put together and executed a five-year plan. We recruited a venture-capital-connected board member and hired an outside CEO with impressive credentials who agreed to remain as CEO once the sale was made so I could exit, ensuring business continuity.

I went on national television to discuss the exit strategy dilemma of small business owners to raise our profile and hopefully attract potential suitors. I vividly recall sitting in that interview chair, nervously trying to attract the interest of the experts we needed without frightening my employees and scaring away customers and prospects who might be watching the program.

The risk paid off. JobBOSS was purchased by a British company in February 1999, but it was a nail-biter up to the last day. The CEO we had hired two years previously for business continuity decided during the last week of contract negotiations that instead of selling to our suitor, he would only stay on if we agreed to an employee buyout. His proposal was rejected by the board of directors, and he abruptly quit. Fortunately, our suitor consummated the sale after I agreed to help them with their other business units for a few years.

Risky business, this risk-taking!

## REWARDS REQUIRE RISKS

Remember Henry, my first programmer? He recently retired at age sixty-five! He stayed with JobBOSS for his entire career—as it was resold over the years and later absorbed by another firm. He and forty-five other key employees had received stock options during my ownership and reaped substantial benefits when we originally sold JobBOSS. Many were able to purchase new homes.

Jack Crowther risked $25,000 and guarantee of a bank line in 1986. In February 1999, his investment risk paid a 3,125 percent return. Jack strayed out of his comfort zone and stepped into the unknown. He took a leap of faith, and as a result, he enjoyed a fun retirement.

If we want to live a life centered on thriving, not just surviving, and achieve our long-term goals, we must take risks. *There is no other way.* Yes, taking risks in life exposes us to potential mistakes, setbacks, and defeats. But Lucille Ball said it well: "I'd rather regret the things that I have done than the things I have not done." By doing something risky, we make room for possibilities and new opportunities. Without taking chances, the probability of achieving anything great is precisely zero.

Everyone fears failure to some degree. By trusting ourselves, we can muster the bravery required to navigate the murky waters of the unknown, build our bridges, and motivate ourselves to reach our goal. It's a hard truth, but achieving anything meaningful requires stepping into the unknown.

## SUCCESS IS NOT LINEAR

Experts recommend creating an actionable plan to get what you want and then fully committing to making it a reality. Taking healthy, calculated risks can be a game changer when it comes to success and goal setting. But big dreams take time to achieve. They involve a lot of grit, hard work, and overcoming obstacles.

Keep in mind that absolutely everyone makes mistakes and falls along the way. Remember the toddler taking her first steps? She will crawl her entire life unless she gets up and tries again. The road to success takes many twists and turns. Thriving may require pivoting and changing direction, traveling unfamiliar paths. If we stubbornly stick to the initial plan, we curb our ability to incorporate what we've learned.

SoulSalt founder Lyn Christian reminds us, "Taking risks can change you fundamentally. They make you braver, stronger, and more confident." She recommends these five steps to take smart and measured risks:[19]

---

19   Lyn Christian, "Taking a Risk in Life."

1. Identify something you want or intend to achieve.
2. Assess the potential risks.
3. Think about the impact of each potential risk.
4. Assign each risk a value.
5. Plan.

## FAILING DOES NOT MAKE YOU A FAILURE

At times, we are all disappointed with our behavior or performance; it's what we do about it that matters. My favorite sportswriter, Kevin Acee of *The San Diego Union-Tribune*, expressed the value of resilience after interviewing San Diego Padre players when they were struggling to win baseball games: "It is important to understand that professional baseball players' *ability to handle failing and know it doesn't make them a failure* is one of the things that sets them apart. That mentality allows them to continue going out in front of thousands of people to try again, time after time."[20]

This observation astounded me. I'm a risk-taker, but I certainly don't have the fortitude to fail at a guaranteed rate of at least 50 percent of the time! Imagine striking out during the bottom of the ninth inning with the bases loaded and being able to suit up, ready to give it another try the next day, day after day, for 162 games a year. That shows incredible belief in one's ability to eventually succeed.

## FAILING RETIREMENT

After I sold JobBOSS, Steve convinced me to move to the Seattle, Washington, area. The girls had graduated from college, and David was in tenth grade. Once again, I was torn, not wanting to move away from the girls but lured by the possibilities of new adventures. I spent the ferry ride between Seattle and Bainbridge Island crying rather than

---

20   Kevin Acee, newsletter, June 21, 2023.

enjoying the spectacular scenery. We had purchased a beautiful home on the bank of Puget Sound with a magnificent view of the Olympic Mountains, and I planned to retire.

I tackled retirement with a vengeance. I planted a huge garden with more than 3,000 flowers, shrubs, and trees. I volunteered with the Seattle YWCA, mentoring teenagers and raising money for their new homeless shelter. I even tried to play golf. Ha! Talk about failing! A golf ball is so little, and a golf club is so long and skinny. I finally realized that golf just ruined a nice stroll through beautiful surroundings. After five years of aimlessly wandering, seeking purpose, I had an epiphany.

## YOU CAN'T BE LUCKY WITHOUT TAKING RISKS

At a New Year's Eve party in December 2007, I was talking to friends about my upcoming trip. They were speechless when I told them that in thirty days, I was flying to Addis Ababa, Ethiopia, by myself, hiring a driver, and going down to South Omo Valley for a month to survey members of the Hamar tribe. No, I didn't have any contacts, and no, I didn't speak the language.

Fortunately, the commander of the US Central Fleet, William Fallon, overheard me and slipped me his business card. He said to call him if I needed any help since Ethiopia was one of the countries he was "responsible for." I emailed him the next day and soon had appointments set up with the US ambassador and the directors of USAID, CARE, and Save the Children.

As the saying goes, I'd rather be lucky than good!

When I decided to work with the Hamar tribe in Ethiopia, I had a four-point plan:

1. Develop a needs assessment survey.
2. Hire a driver and translator.

3. Pack provisions and camp in South Omo Valley for forty days, asking questions and listening.
4. Analyze the survey results and figure out the next step.

I needed to learn what I didn't know before I could decide what programs needed to be implemented. And then, someway, somehow, the programs needed to be funded. I had no idea what risks and opportunities awaited me. Stay tuned.

## Flying to the Moon

Ella Madison grew up in a house filled with fear, prevented from taking risks of any kind or disappearing from her single mom's sight. Being an imaginative and energetic only child, Ella discovered that by living in "the land of make-believe," she was free to do whatever she wanted. For eight years, Ella had fun conversations and adventures with a lot of imaginary siblings, going on magic carpet rides across America and flying to the moon. Her adventurous pretend family was replaced with a real baby brother shortly after her mom married. Although Ella was no longer the focus of her mom's obsessive attention, she still wasn't allowed to go places, visit friends, or participate in events without her mom's strict supervision.

When she was in eighth grade, she wrote to NASA and suggested a rocket design she thought might work. They didn't write back.

Ella took a major risk and moved to Florida's Space Coast for college, the furthest point from home. She had no experience being on her own, not even for a night, and had never used an ATM or ridden a public bus. Ella didn't let her fear of the unknown stop her. Instead, she seized the opportunity to go to the best college possible to learn how to build her rocket. She took classes nonstop, and at barely twenty-three, with a BS in astrophysics and astronomy and a master's in space systems in hand, she landed a job with a leading space company. Ella is now a well-respected rocket engineer preparing for her next stop: flying to the moon and beyond.

## FEAR IS POWERFUL

Why does it seem so natural to take risks in some areas and yet so difficult to take risks in other areas? Why did I feel comfortable taking significant risks in my professional life yet remain hesitant to divorce Steve?

During my first fifty years, I took risks when I glimpsed new opportunities, and that vision propelled me forward. I had not yet learned to use fear as my source of power. That would require asking for help, which was foreign territory. It meant admitting that I had a weakness and couldn't do everything alone.

In "retirement," I was once again a toddler, learning how to navigate a new world.

# DREAM:
## *Taking Risks to Explore New Opportunities*

**D**esire: Embrace new adventures (and risks) to learn and grow.

**R**eflect on the opportunities I currently forfeit because I am afraid of taking risk.

**E**xplore the root cause of my fear(s).

**A**cknowledge that I might fail and that a backup plan might give me the courage to try.

**M**antra:
My courageous spirit wants to fly.
My childlike spirit intuits the truth.
My wise woman within holds my hand.

### WISE WOMAN WORDS

*"You gain strength, courage, and confidence by every experience in which you really stop to look fear in the face."*
—Eleanor Roosevelt

# 8

# Asking for Help

Some people find it easy to ask for help, while others consider it unbearably complicated and difficult. Just like we are born to take risks, we are born to ask for help. It's human nature. In fact, screaming for help at the top of our lungs is the first thing we do when we leave the warmth and nurturing comfort of Mother's womb. Arms flailing, face scrunched up, wailing while we gasp for air. Instinctively, we cry for help. So why do we stop asking when we lack the ability to help ourselves? What changes?

Something shifts for those of us who become reluctant and uncomfortable. Asking no longer feels safe and acceptable. For many, that acquired reluctance or fear comes from the way we were brought up. Others experience trauma along the way. Some of us have low self-esteem and feel that we do not deserve someone else's time and energy. Others' inner critics mire them in shame, leaving them to feel it's their duty to pull themselves up by their bootstraps.

If you're like me, your childhood experiences and environment taught you that it was unsafe and unacceptable to have your needs met. Neglect and abuse decimate a child's sense of worth and identity and instill negative core beliefs. People who have endured abuse often try to be invisible by making very few demands.

I felt safe when I was able to camouflage my limitations. The sharper my survival skills became, the more trouble I had asking for help. I was able to share experiences, offering facts and opinions, but I did not allow myself to become vulnerable, and no one was allowed to breach my body armor—until I met Bill (part 4).

## LEARNING TO ASK

A cop and a chaplain were standing outside when I answered our door at midnight on November 3, 2002. They told us that we had to leave for Seattle immediately, that the ferry was being held for us. My son, David, had experienced a horrible accident, and the doctors didn't expect him to make it through the night. He had been driving his car on Bainbridge Island when he hit a patch of black ice. His car flipped on its top and spun in circles for fifty yards. Wedged in the driver's seat, David suffered a traumatic brain injury and basal skull fractures. His left arm was mangled, and his optic chiasm and pituitary gland were damaged. Fortunately, his friend immediately called for help, and David was flown by helicopter to Harborview Medical Center in Seattle.

We were lucky. We had the best doctors, and since I was retired, I could make sure that the eleven different services working on the various bits and pieces of David knew what the others were doing. Six weeks later, after five major surgeries, we were able to bring him home. I was 100 percent focused on his long road to recovery and had no idea how traumatized I was by my fear of losing him.

David's recovery was a painful, twisting journey—emotionally, psychologically, and physically. I am so proud of the man he has become. He is a wonderful dad, a loving husband, and a caring son. What a testament to the resilience of the human spirit! The bumps in his path gave me the opportunity to start healing myself.

While attending his family week at the Sierra Tucson rehab center (addiction to pain pills are a bitch), I heard about EMDR (eye movement desensitization and reprocessing) therapy. It was devised by Francine Shapiro in 1987 to alleviate the distress associated with traumatic memories, such as in the case of post-traumatic stress disorder (PTSD). Through a series of guided visualizations, the graphic memory stored on the right side of the brain is transferred to the left side of the brain as an "intellectualized" memory.

Once back in the Seattle area, with the help of an excellent EMDR therapist, I was able to effectively process David's accident and my childhood "You are the devil" event. I still remember both, but I am no longer retraumatized every time I think about them.

I was impressed with Sierra Tucson's rehab program and thrilled to learn that they offered a trauma track designed to help people suffering from PTSD and abuse. I signed up and self-enrolled in October 2005. It was the best thing I ever did for me. I was forced to focus entirely on myself and learned so much. Since we only had access to books in their bookstore, I decided to learn about shame-based family systems and surrogate wives. Wow! Both were shocking. What eye-openers.

I had never heard of the theory of shame-based family systems until I was encouraged to research it. John Bradshaw outlines the rules that govern shame-based families in his book *Healing the Shame That Binds You*:[21]

- Perfectionism: Always be right in everything you do.
- Blame: Whenever things don't turn out as planned, blame yourself or others.
- It is wrong to think, feel, or desire anything different from what you are told to think, feel, and desire.
- Don't make mistakes.
- Don't trust anyone and you will never be disappointed.

What a lousy way to live, having someone else control your interactions, feelings, and personal behavior. And yet that was my generational family system. When I came to realize this at age fifty-

---

21   John Bradshaw, *Healing the Shame That Binds You* (Health Communications Inc., 2005).

five, I thought it was too late to change the impact this had made on my kids. I hoped there was still time to interrupt the trajectory of my grandchildren's lives. I desperately wanted them to have healthy self-esteem and to feel worthy of love.

Several weeks into the program, my therapist announced that I was going to be blindfolded for the next few days. She had determined that I needed to learn how to ask for help. I felt like I had been sentenced to death by lethal injection. The mere idea of not being in charge of where I was in relation to my environment terrified me. Cold sweats. Chills. Extreme anxiety.

Once the ordeal began, I was gobsmacked. I loved not having to make decisions. Someone was always there, ready to take my hand and lead me wherever I needed to go. I enjoyed trusting others, content to just show up. This exercise was just what I needed. My therapist was spot-on.

I learned that asking for help is *not* a sign of weakness. It still does not come easily to me, but I have found that it improves my relationships, particularly with my kids. They love it when I allow them to help me in some way.

## WHY IS ASKING SO HARD?

Much has been written about the challenges of asking for help. The root cause appears to be fear. Since fear keeps us from growing and realizing our potential, let's refer to a 2023 article in the *Harvard Business Review*, "Why It's So Hard to Ask for Help," by Manfred F. R. Kets de Vries, professor of leadership, where he explores four of our major fears and how to convert them into positive action:

1. *Fear of being vulnerable.*

For people who are insecure and preoccupied with others' perceptions of them, asking for help feels like a sign of weakness.

They're afraid that it will make them look incompetent and inferior.

WebMD suggests that to overcome the fear of being vulnerable, we need self-compassion. Remind yourself how brave you are to be vulnerable, no matter how small it seems at the moment. Try to avoid focusing on other people's opinions. Slow down. Be present.

2. *Fear of being dependent.*

Hyperindependence is a coping mechanism that develops because of negative experiences. It teaches us that relying on and trusting others is not safe. Sometimes, family and cultural backgrounds cause people to believe they should be capable of handling everything by themselves, programmed to play the Lone Ranger. Independence is critical to their self-image.

In the Choosing Therapy newsletter, Silvi Saxena, a social worker, oncology social worker, and clinical trauma professional, recommends that taking time to work through trust issues is essential. Allow people you know to care about you. Practice saying no when you feel overwhelmed by the needs of others. Give yourself the gift of saving your energy for when *you* need it.

3. *Fear of losing control.*

This is the fear that something terrible will happen if we do not control the outcome of future events. People who consistently suffer from a fear of losing control remain in a state of anxiety with only brief breaks between episodes.

Elliot D. Cohen, PhD, writes in *Psychology Today* that the crux of this fear is the demand for certainty in a world that is tentative and uncertain. It is precisely this unrealistic demand that creates the anxiety. We think that we *must* accurately predict and manage the future, not just have some probable and uncertain handle on it.

The key to overcoming this fear is to work on letting go of the demand for certainty. It is we who must concede; reality won't ever give up its uncertainty for us.

4. *Fear of rejection.*

This is closely related to the fear of being vulnerable. Many people who struggle with low self-esteem, lack of confidence, shame, or guilt spend a lot of time and energy worrying about what others think of them. They are often people pleasers and take on too many responsibilities. Many fear that asking for help will cause them to be abandoned or disliked.

Michelle Risser, in her Choosing Therapy article "Fear of Rejection: Signs, Effects, & How to Overcome," recommends first trying to accept that we fear rejection and to simply notice that it's there. She encourages us to build the habit of positive self-talk by repeating a simple mantra like "I am enough" or "I can do hard things."

Don't let rejection define you. Every person is unique and special, and each has their own gifts. Remember that just because you are afraid of rejection doesn't mean you have to let that fear be a part of your identity.

## THREAT OF DROWNING FOCUSES THE MIND

In 2007, when I founded Global Team for Local Initiatives (GTLI), a nonprofit 501(c)(3), I thought, *What's the big deal?* I started JobBOSS when I had no managerial experience, just sales and bookkeeping. This time around, I already knew how to work with a board of directors, manage people, develop strategic plans, and build teams. Piece of cake.

Talk about being arrogant and naive.

Starting an international charity in a third-world country run by a dictatorship masquerading as a democracy—whose strategy to prevent unemployment (over 40 percent) is to penalize companies that terminate incompetent employees—is a whole different matter. Not to mention all the bureaucratic hurdles to jump and the quicksand pits to navigate. I was so focused on helping the Hamar that I refused to acknowledge that I was energetically sinking further underwater.

I was fortunate that my founding board members were professionals: an epidemiologist who had worked in Ethiopia for fifty years, a retired Stanford professor with extensive food economics experience in developing countries, and a former JobBOSS board member who knew me well. Thanks to Commander Bill Fallon, I had top-level contacts in the US foreign-aid donor community, and with the dedicated help of a tiny American team, our network of supporting rotary clubs kept growing. Externally, things appeared to be going well. However, I was missing a key component.

I had no higher power.

Since rejecting my childhood belief system in my early fifties, I'd relied on science for answers. That worked okay until I was living in Ethiopia by myself, expending tremendous amounts of energy to help the less fortunate. I had no "refill mechanism" to recharge my batteries. My positive energy flowed out, but the only energy coming in was negative (anger at the corruption and abuse of power). I had not yet learned how to convert negative energy into positive power. Still hyperindependent and wanting to be in control, I was the Lone Ranger.

## TRANSATLANTIC INFUSION OF HELP

Fortunately, I had a good experience asking for help at Sierra Tucson. Surviving those three days of stumbling around blindfolded proved it was okay to be dependent on others. Now, three years later, over 8,000 miles from home and struggling to catch my breath, I had an epiphany that introduced me to my higher power.

One extremely hot day in March 2009, more than 200 people crowded around me for hours, frantic to receive a pill. Since 86 percent of the people in South Omo Valley were suffering from waterborne disease (intestinal worms) and 92 percent from communicable disease, everyone felt lousy and wanted medicine. When the crowd saw one individual get a blue pill, everyone asked, "What did you say?" and then the next person repeated the same ailment to get the blue pill.

The women were draped in goatskin. The top was basically the body of a small goat hanging down the front of the torso, partially covering the breasts. The skirt was another goatskin, with a longer tail in the back that the wearer pulled between her legs when squatting on her haunches. Women mixed red clay and butter together and rubbed it into twisted strands of hair. The men wore dirty shorts or loincloths. No one bathed, and the temperature was over 100 degrees.

The combination of the smell of goatskin and unwashed bodies and the extreme heat overwhelmed me. I started feeling faint, staggered to my feet, and was led to a mattress under a tree. Marmaru, the tribe's medicine man, sat next to me, quietly giving me strength to continue.

A few months before, my somatic therapist, Sharon Stanley, shared with me the pronouncement made by the shaman at her spiritual retreat center, Eastern Star, in Brazil. When Sharon showed Henrique a picture of a young Hamar girl, he spent three hours asking her about specific aspects of my work and impressed on her that I had to have courage and faith. He felt that my mission was supreme and enlightened and came from the depths of my heart. He promised that he and his Umbanda community would send me strength and guidance whenever I asked for it.

That March night, in the quiet of my tent, I called Sharon on my satellite phone to ask her to let Henrique know I was in desperate need of that promised support. The next morning, I woke up full of optimism, raring to go; I had received a bolt of energy. Here I was in one of the remotest areas of Africa, and a community in Brazil had sent me strength. A true out-of-body experience.

Sharon had first discovered Eastern Star several years before, on a poster advertising one of their spiritual retreats. She took a risk. She decided to explore new opportunities and traveled to the remote center outside of Belo Horizonte, Brazil. The Eastern Star community loosely follows the religious practice of Umbanda, a syncretic Afro-Brazilian religion that blends traditional African practices with Roman

Catholicism, spiritism, and Indigenous American beliefs. The history of Umbanda can be traced back to the slave trade, when West African peoples were unwillingly uprooted with no belongings but their traditions and beliefs. Over the years, beliefs of the West Africans, their colonial masters, and the Indigenous natives of South America were mixed and melded into their own unique religion: Umbanda. This practice has a focus on communication between spirits and the living. Spirits can be called upon through rituals and can intervene in people's lives.

As the saying goes, desperate people do desperate things, and that night in South Omo, I was desperate. During the year after the "forgotten not stolen" medicine bag incident, word had spread that an older *ferengi* (anyone who is not Black) lady was handing out free medicine, and Hamar were walking miles in the hot sun to see me. I was in danger, both with the Hamar and the government. The Hamar tribe was suffering, dying from dehydration caused by ascaris (intestinal worms), which causes chronic diarrhea. The cure, mebendazole, was readily available at the health center in Turmi, but the lady in charge demanded a bribe to sell me more blue pills. I was determined *not* to pay bribes to anyone. Besides, I had no more cash stashed in my backpack (no ATMs available).

Major dilemma. No more pills. Sick people who walked miles in the hot sun seeking relief were being turned away. I was exhausted. The tribesmen were pissed. My support team was rapidly disappearing. You bet I needed energy. The irony didn't even register with me at the time; I was eager to receive energy transmitted from strangers on the other side of the world when I had scoffed at the "faith healing" events that happened every Sunday at my mother's church. Eventually, I rationalized that the energy I was connected to is based on spirituality rather than the dogma of a particular organized religion.

## INSATIABLE CURIOSITY

I wanted more bolts of energy. How could I get them? Six months later, Sharon arranged for a group of somatic therapists to participate in a special spiritual retreat at Eastern Star, and I tagged along. I was excited to meet Henrique, but I was scared. The only way to keep getting those energy bolts was to immerse myself in this "weird stuff," and I kept having flashbacks of my mother's behavior: speaking in tongues, slain in the Lord (her term for falling down and losing consciousness), etc. I told myself that this was different, but I was emotionally spooked.

Our group drove for several hours from Belos to the remote and serene retreat center. Walking single file down a narrow path, we heard singing and clapping. Suddenly, there he was, Henrique, walking toward us, followed by *cubukos*—people under a spell—dressed in costumes, dancing, jumping high in the air before falling to their knees, and drawing back phantom arrows and aiming them at the sky. I'd never seen anything like it.

They led us to a clearing filled with a congregation of people chanting and singing to the beat of drums. After Henrique completed his homily in Portuguese, the cubukos spread out in a circle, paying homage and allegiance to him. Henrique directed individual members to specific cubukos, who appeared to give them advice and a blessing. Suddenly, it was our turn. I was directed to the snake lady, a commanding, heavyset woman who had draped a large fake snake around her shoulders. She shared how I was filled with negative energy that needed to be pulled out of my body. Sergio, Henrique's translator, stood at my shoulder, murmuring words of comfort. Curious, I decided to go with the flow and see what happened.

That week transformed my life. Henrique knew everything about me. He knew that I had been reincarnated many times and was shocked that I had been roaming the earth longer than he had. He urged me to concentrate on my present life and to simply accept that I had past lives. He said a big ceremony was planned for me on Saturday. He wanted the elders of Eastern Star present so he could draw on their energy.

The purpose of Saturday's ceremony was to get rid of the negative energy I brought from Africa. He wanted me balanced and nurtured when I left. He could "see" that guides had accompanied me from Africa as protection and wanted to make sure they felt welcome.

What an elaborate ceremony. Goats suddenly appeared. There was gruel making, beating of drums, singing, chanting, and piles of offerings. Over fifty people participated, many of them "incorporated" (transformed) into cubukos—some cowboys, some childlike spirits. It became a dizzying array of movement and sound.

I was pulled into the middle of the circle, whirling, twirling, losing my balance, at times on my knees with the dry heaves. I'm sure I was in a trance. When it felt like the Hamar beads around my neck were choking me, loving hands removed them. I felt the community's intense care and concern for my safety.

When it was over, I felt like I had been pulled into the nurturing bosom of everyone there. My energy felt loved, balanced, like the essence of me had been understood and my soul had been mended. I was told that I would feel the presence of that energy infusion, comfort, and support for seven years, and I did. I became acquainted with my spirit guides: Oxum is my wise woman, Oxossi is my warrior, and Eres is my playful imp.

By the end of the ceremony, I was all in. I wanted Henrique's help with every aspect of my life, starting with my relationship with my kids. He helped me understand that I had insulated myself from them. It was like I had a moat around me with a bridge I could pull up. Whenever I didn't know how to deal with a situation, I retreated. I was so afraid of being an enabler that I wasn't emotionally available. With Henrique's help, I slowly lowered the drawbridge, thawed out, and was able to feel my children's love for me and my profound love for them. Soon after, I purchased a family home near them in Minnesota where we could gather when I was in the States.

Our family history of unsatisfactory marriages continued to manifest. In 2009, Shay, David, and I all filed for divorce. Melissa got married that summer but divorced ten years later. We were all continuing down a well-worn path, only this time we had the courage (and cultural permission) to divorce rather than staying in unsatisfying, unhappy relationships. My fervent prayer for my grandchildren is that we have successfully interrupted the pattern and they will find healthy, well-grounded partners.

## HELP ME!

Ethiopia is a fascinating country, home to eighty-six tribes. The capital city, Addis Ababa, is the headquarters of the African Union. The country receives significant foreign aid and attention due to its strategic location and relative stability. The smartest, best-educated Ethiopians are hired as managers by the hundreds of embassies and offices of large nongovernment organizations (NGOs). It was tough for GTLI, a small, poorly funded start-up, to compete for qualified employees.

I was often overwhelmed and struggled to determine the next step. At times, the challenges in Addis Ababa felt insurmountable. The political machinations, corruption, petty bureaucracy, inefficiency, unnecessary roadblocks, and bottlenecks wore me down. With so many emotional and intellectual frustrations, I played down the physical inconveniences, such as electricity disappearing for days at a time, having to filter all my water (when it was available), stepping over donkey manure, and the constant noise—people loudly talking and competing religious broadcasts blasting their amplifiers.

Living in Addis filled my body with irritation and anger at the relentless chaos and constant communication struggles, at straining to understand and be understood, at the inefficiencies and paranoia. Whenever the government felt mobile phones and the internet were being used to spread discontent, communication sources were shut down.

My not having a college degree was a major issue for the Ethiopian government. How could anyone be qualified to run an NGO without a college degree? Whenever we terminated an incompetent employee, the employee complained to the licensing office. For years, we appeased them with my high school National Honor Society certificate.

JobBOSS was successful because we were fierce competitors. At GTLI, we had to prove that we were the opposite—effective collaborators. Donors wanted us to work with the local government workers, who unfortunately were accustomed to receiving bribes from other NGOs. Our policy from day one was no bribes and no paying per diem to encourage learning. Until we became recognized as the leading NGO in South Omo, legions of local government extension workers (health, agriculture, education) worked to undermine our programs.

I often fell asleep murmuring, "Help me, help me, help me."

### 1, 2, 3, 4 AND MAGIC APPEARS

Thanks to Eastern Star teaching me how to ask for and receive help, I began to wake up feeling refreshed and full of new ideas. I developed a process:

First, make a conscious decision to open my mind by acknowledging the need for assistance. Admit that I am unable to do "it" alone. Be vulnerable. Be dependent. Give up control.

Second, physically say, "Please help me." Asking freely for help means I accept my limitations. I have to believe I deserved help.

Third, actively listen, pay attention, and seriously evaluate the response to my request. Process and accept the help being offered.

Fourth, act on the advice received. Grab hold of the helping hand and allow my guides to lead me. Let them help solve the dilemma of the day.

## Asking Is Magical

After more than twenty years of marriage to her high school sweetheart, Molly thought life was good. The hard work she and her husband invested in getting him an engineering degree had paid off—until the day he announced he had fallen in love with someone else. Boom, he disappeared, refusing to pay child support or the mortgage. Even though Molly had always worked, most of her jobs paid minimum wage. She couldn't even qualify for a credit card, much less pay a mortgage. Suddenly Molly and her girls were homeless.

Fortunately, a friend who needed help running his tennis facility offered her a free apartment, a stipend, and the chance to give occasional tennis lessons. Every $25 lesson bought the groceries. During the next five years, Molly asked everyone she met whether they needed a secretary. Finally, Bob, a writer for a consulting company, said yes. Molly immediately called for an interview, and early the next morning, dolled up in her best outfit—nylons, high heels, the works—she met Frank, the big boss, who was wearing baggy shorts and flip-flops, looking like he had just waded out of the water.

Frank and his partner spent less than five minutes interviewing Molly. She was asking for pennies, and they said no. They had to pay her more because paying her so little would be too embarrassing. That was the longest conversation she remembers having with either of them for years. No one talked to her for several months, no direction was given, barely a good morning or good night spoken. Molly, earning more than she ever imagined possible, started opening file boxes, organizing, asking other employees questions, and learning, desperate to keep the job. She was the first to arrive and last to leave, fearful that each week might be her last. Over time, her confidence grew. During campaign season, Frank and his partner would disappear for months, leaving Molly in charge. Twenty-seven years later, she retired from the best decision she ever made for her life and for her children: saying yes to those two extraordinary men during that unusual interview.

Molly counsels her grandkids to say yes. Someday, they too might meet someone who could change their lives. Molly still says yes to most things. Now eighty-two years old, she wants to enjoy as many new experiences as possible.

## BUILDING MUSCLE MEMORY

I decided to follow the advice in Malcolm Gladwell's book *Outliers: The Story of Success* and practice asking for help and reciting my mantra 10,000 times so that both would become natural for me.

Honestly, I think I have hit the 10,000 mark for the mantra aspect. I desperately want to "renew in my being the endless source of peace, love, and harmony." I haven't become a master of it yet, though—not by a long shot. My impatience is such a tall hurdle, and I can never quite get over it. Henrique has assured me that what needs to be done for me to reach where I am meant to be will happen: *Don't be concerned. The guides are at work. Have faith and relax into it.*

I still have another 9,000 times to go with regard to asking for help. It was easy to ask in Ethiopia because I was constantly overwhelmed—dealing with the people in power in Addis Ababa and seeing what was happening to people with no power in the field. Now, living in the States, old habits of relying on myself kick in.

Whether we are guided by religious or spiritual beliefs, a neighbor, a boss, or some undetermined inner voice, when we allow ourselves to be vulnerable and ask for help, we open the door for growth. Fortunately, we don't have to be perfect to find purpose and feel fulfilled. We grow when we open our minds to think new thoughts and dream new dreams, but this requires stimuli. Read on for new ideas and fresh avenues to explore.

Each of us is worthy of being valued. Of being unfettered and free.

# DREAM:
## *Asking for Help*

**D**esire: Acknowledge my limitations so I may learn from others.

**R**eflect on who has the experience and ability to help me.

**E**xplore how I can best access and receive their counsel.

**A**cknowledge that I need to park my pride outside and be ready to act on the help received.

**M**antra:
To trust, I need to let go.
To learn, I need to make mistakes.
To grow, I need to stay awkward.

### WISE WOMAN WORDS

"Asking for help doesn't make you weak; it makes you wise."
—Michelle Obama

# PART THREE

## Set Yourself Free

I grew up believing in the American Dream. If I worked hard, with great determination and initiative, I would be successful and happy. When I achieved the dream, I wasn't happy, and I certainly didn't feel at peace. Others deemed me successful because I no longer needed to work, but I felt bored and unfulfilled. There was still fear to overcome, early programming to rewrite, risks to take, and learning to be done.

Setting ourselves free from mental, physical, and cultural attachments that hinder our personal growth is a life changer. The benefits vastly outweigh the effort required to drum up the courage and scrub our personal beliefs and values. We gain the power to align our actions with the moral compass we have defined. We become free to pursue our passions and dreams.

Breaking free is not easy, but it is doable. The next four chapters discuss how to gain purpose and direction. They present a road map to diversifying, exploring how cultural constraints influence your choices, and gaining insight by reflecting on experiences that expand your ability to empathize and feel compassion, and they encourage you to empower and build self-sustaining capabilities in others.

# 9

# Learning from "Different" People and Cultures

When we see an eye doctor, we read the chart, look through the gizmo while a technician flips the lenses, choose A or B, and then some of us walk out with a prescription for new glasses. Suddenly, images become sharper, and colors are brighter.

Imagine going to a cultural lens doctor. You sit in a chair, look through the gizmo, and a technician flips through your biases and prejudices. You contemplate each one and think, *Yeah, that makes sense. My view of the world is right.* Of course, it feels that way because you have been programmed from birth, influenced by your education and experience, reinforced by the news you absorb and what you Google. What you watch, read, and pay attention to defines how you think. Without considering foreign customs and social mores—norms of morality and right and wrong—in their cultural context, it is difficult to internalize and accept any differences. You ask yourself, *Why would people do that? Think like that? Behave like that? Put up with that?*

Beware! The same old same old stagnates. New and different stimulates.

It's tough to think outside the box if we never leave it—if we're talking to the same people, visiting the same places, and doing the same things over and over. Stuck in the same paradigm, same perspective, same set of ideas, same way of looking at things.

Unlocking our minds to think new thoughts and dream new dreams requires stimuli. By questioning and exploring processes, systems, and ideas, we uncover truths, and the process of realizing these truths opens new paths, which lead to new thoughts, allowing our journeys to continue.

Innovation and change only happen when we are willing to poke around the edges of familiarity. Smelling new aromas and fragrances, hearing different beats and rhythms, seeing the way others interact and conduct their business, and feeling the ebb and flow of daily living all broaden our world of possibilities.

## SHIFTING MY PARADIGMS

During the Rwandan genocide, when over 800,000 people were massacred in 100 days in 1994, I was lost in a workaholic haze, unable to process the horror I was seeing on TV. I didn't have the mind space. I could only wonder how powerless people coped when terrible atrocities struck, violently disrupting their lives. Suddenly, through no fault of their own, their survival was at stake. What were they supposed to do? Where could they live?

Retired at forty-nine and no longer working an insane number of hours, I had the time and resources to search for answers. But first, my husband Steve insisted we go to Antarctica, his ultimate bucket-list trip. Surprise! I had never even thought about Antarctica, but what the heck, why not? We started checking out expedition travel companies and found the perfect match: small ship (100 passengers), well-regarded lecturers, expert leaders, and interesting fellow adventurers. We thoroughly enjoyed the experience, and I was amazed by what I learned. Hooked, for the next seven years we spent a month a year exploring remote areas of Asia, Africa, and South America. I was like a sponge, absorbing what I saw, smelled, heard, and touched. I started imagining living another person's life, viewing the world through their eyes. My perspective changed. What I discovered was very different from what I had been taught in school.

Being treated like a monkey in a cage in Chad gave me pause, experiencing discrimination in Ethiopia increased my empathy, and diving deep under the sea filled me with wonder. These experiences shifted my paradigms. A cultural optometrist had fine-tuned my cultural lens, and my view of the world came into focus. I started to schedule free time to sit and reflect, to absorb and integrate new ways of thinking. It was an exciting and invigorating process. Each of these paradigm shifts (PS) deepened my conviction about the importance of understanding context.

## PS #1: WE EVOLVED; SCIENCE WINS
### *Head Out of the Sand*

It was a mega-sin for my sisters and I to even contemplate evolution. Eve was created from Adam's rib, and when Eve took a bite of the fateful apple, the big "sin" happened. Evolution? Not possible. The mere thought was blasphemy to the highest degree. Mother would not just roll over in her grave; we would hear her screaming, along with millions of others who share her belief system.

The history books in my highly rated Midwestern public school likewise ignored historical truths proven by archeological discoveries in Asia, Africa, and South America. The whys and outcomes of key events were often tinted and glossed over to align with popular societal beliefs. We need to voice our concern about the books being banned today; attempts to rewrite history are still happening before our very eyes!

Check out the artifacts in the museums of China and India, the Egyptian relics, and the strong jaw lines and teeth of people today who eat meat without utensils. Explore the remote areas of the world that have little access to modern conveniences or the internet. Because let me tell you, the scientists got it right. Evolution is real. I know this to be true because I had the good fortune to witness it in Patagonia and the Amazonian basin and in Ethiopia.

### *Starting to Dig*

My quest to understand the truth about human nature and the beginning of mankind began in earnest at the tail end of our 2001 Antarctic expedition (highly recommended). We were visiting the cave of the mastodon in Tierra del Fuego, Patagonia, when I saw concrete proof that evolution was an indisputable reality. Time and again, it became apparent that much of what I had been programmed to believe was just *wrong*. My search for answers accelerated as I dug into anthropology and studied Indigenous cultures. Exploring the five major rivers of the Amazonian basin clearly revealed how the evolution of species occurred. Spending time in the bush in twelve African countries exposed me to cultures untouched by modern societies.

### *Baboon Face-off*

Baboons think and behave like several humans I know. I was startled by how much the facial expressions and body language of the huge baboon resembled one of my former sales managers while he stole my breakfast one sunny morning in Arba Minch, Ethiopia. My table was next to a three-foot-high concrete barrier, separating the dining area from a large, terraced viewing area. I was admiring the view of Lake Chamu and Lake Abaya, listening to the birds, and enjoying my macchiato and bread. Suddenly, a burly, gigantic baboon jumped down next to me, stared me in the eyes, and defiantly grabbed my bread. I could tell he was thinking about taking my macchiato, so I acted fast. I gave him my most defiant look in return (false bravado in the face of terror), grabbed my drink, and surrendered my table. He won. He was bigger, and his nails were much sharper.

### *Unexpected Discovery*

One unexpected free day in Agadez, Niger, I said yes to one of the guides and ended up with an unbelievable experience. Several of us piled into an old Land Rover and headed out across the hot, barren Sahara Desert with no GPS or discernible (to me, at least) landmarks. We drove for hours. Occasionally, we saw a shack or two or a young child pulling a reluctant camel through the endless sea of sand. Suddenly, in the middle of nowhere, we stopped by a blanket hanging from a scraggly tree. Next to our vehicle was a large circle of stones. Inside the circle was a fossilized Tyrannosaurus rex next to a brontosaurus, both partially covered by sand. It looked like they had battled to the death. Alongside was a giant prehistoric crocodile surrounded by several smaller dinosaurs. All these creatures had been caught in the great floods of the Sahara basin 135 million years ago. The oldest human remains found to date are 233,000 years old. Science is indisputable when you see the facts.

## PS #2: POLYGAMY WORKS
### *Say What?!*

Polygamy provides a solution to fundamental problems in some cultures. I never thought I'd ever type that sentence, let alone believe it to be true. No way. Bad! Bad! Mother would not approve. Truth is, polygamy basically works in Hamar, and it works for the Biakan pygmies of the Central African Republic.

The happiest people I have ever observed are the Biakan pygmies. Biakan life is communal. They have no exclusive nor permanent relationships. Men and women pair off indiscriminately at night according to their mutual desires. Babies are born and raised by the community. There are no defined families. Unfortunately, the Biakan pygmies are close to extinction, their hunting grounds decimated by lumber companies. It's horrible for them and a real shame for us. They have amassed so much wisdom.

### *Benefits of Being First*

In my early days working in Hamar, seeing elders with multiple wives made me angry. Angry at the elders and sad for the women. Eventually I paused and took a breath and started to observe the interaction between the women in the elder's compound. Shocking as this may sound, polygamy saved many of these women from literally dying from overwork. When a young virgin was added to the communal family, the burden on the other wives lessened. It was the youngest woman's job to service the elder and have the babies. She was the strongest, so she often carried the heaviest load. The older women cooked and watched the children. The older the wife, the happier she was. I decided that if I were Hamar, I would want to be first wife, even though that would mean my iron collar would have a protuberance under my chin.

My friend Dobe Oita is a first wife.

The wives were kind and considerate to each other. They washed each other's backs at the water pump. They dressed each other's hair by swirling strands of it with clay and butter. Most seemed friendly with each other, but there was jealousy. My friend Guido Oita pleaded with me to help her have children. She was the first wife of the most important elder of the clan, Bali Sudo, and because she only had two children, Bali married a younger wife and no longer slept with her.

## PS #3: COLLABORATION OR COMPETITION?
### *For the Good of the Group*

One day, I had the incredible opportunity to go hunting with the Biakan pygmies. As early as eight years old, girls start weaving hunting nets out of stringy tree bark. The nets end up being about four feet high and twenty to forty feet long. (These people come up to my waist.) The community hunts together for duiker, a small antelope that hides in dense bush. As soon as spotters identify likely hiding spots, the hunting party spreads out the nets between bushes. Everyone starts to beat the bush with their sticks, yelling to drive a spooked duiker into their net. The captured duiker's tiny leg is promptly broken before it is awarded to the female who owns the net.

### *Karma's a B!*

The hunt I witnessed took forever; the nets were set and the bushes whacked repeatedly that morning. It was so hot and humid that I felt like I was crying from the sweat running down my face and back, with the bees and bugs darting at me, trying to drink it. Yuk! Frustrated by their lack of success, the hunting party huddled together and decided to change their luck by asking a certain man to drop out of the hunt. The man scuttled off into a small cluster of trees. He smiled and waved at us when we shuffled by. Later, we learned the community elders decided this man was causing their bad luck. Evidently, he had misbehaved in some way the previous evening and therefore negatively affected the hunt's karma. Sure enough, the next time the hunters started yelling and beating the bush, a tiny little duiker ran into the net.

### *Me Versus You*

Our Western world is built on competition. Winners receive more money and recognition. We start competing before we even go to school. We vie for attention from Mom and Dad, racing our best friends, playing soccer, T-ball, jacks, board games, and word games, participating in spelling bees, and taking quizzes and tests.

The only reason I was able to travel and experience all these cool things is that I was a lucky competitor. Yep, luck plays a huge part in success. One of my good friends started a business the same time I started JobBOSS. She worked just as many hours. She was a much better networker than me. The big difference between my success and her failure was that I chose an underserved market niche and was luckier in early situations. When I had no idea what I was doing, I guessed and rolled the dice.

### *Maybe I Don't Have to Be the Best*

I was in my fifties before my self-perception could handle not being the best: best swimmer, best salesperson, best small business owner, best mom (oops, that didn't quite happen). I never dreamed that collaboration might be more effective than competition until I observed other cultures and the genuine caring and kindness Indigenous women showed in fetching dirty water from deep holes dug in the sand, nursing each other's babies, and sharing heavy loads, always committed to keeping each other alive.

### *Perhaps Collaborating Is the Answer*

Remember reading about the old barn-raising days when neighbors got together to build someone's barn? I have only witnessed true collaborative efforts of this nature in third-world countries. The homeless appear to collaborate at times in urban America, but not those of us who live in our safe little cocoons, keeping watch and building barriers to make sure no one invades our space. I wonder if that's why depression has become so prevalent among the wealthy and the suicide rate is rising so quickly—the pressure of competition, the isolation, the noncommunal nature of American life today. Something to consider: Collaboration may be better than competition.

## PS #4: SPIRITUALITY MATTERS, NOT RELIGION
### *A Higher Power*

People experience joy and receive comfort from myriad forms of worship, including organized religions such as Christianity, Judaism, Islam, Hindu, Buddhism, even Voodoo. Others are happy being atheist or agnostic. Some prefer spiritualism; some participate in ancestral worship. Others believe in animism, and many subscribe to science.

### *The Evils of Mind Control*

During my travels, I saw evidence that one of the worst things to happen to Africa was organized religion. Foreign armies came and conquered land and grabbed resources. To control the people, however, they needed to control their minds. One of the first things they did was introduce a new religion. Some historians refer to religion as slavery of the mind—an artificial structure that allows people in power to manipulate and control. Structured religion often furnishes a lens through which people view their lives and their places within society. It provides a perceived "safe" understanding of the world, a structure that defines right and wrong, good and evil. It provides a framework, rules to follow to "ensure" you go where you want when you die.

Some believe that spirituality is for people who have been to hell and don't want to go back, so they strive to access wisdom greater than their own to help them find purpose. Some folks feel religion is for people who don't want to go to hell in the first place, so they choose to follow a road map that helps them prepare for life after death.

I think belief in a higher power is the difference maker. Accessing some source of wisdom and nurturing that is greater than ourselves provides comfort. Personally, I find solace in asking my spirit guides for help. They always answer my call. My daughter prays to God—and her call is answered as well.

## PS #5: YOUR PURPOSE IS SITTING THERE; GRAB IT

In 2007, I was in Timia, Niger, when a little girl of about six years—the same age as my granddaughter Ella—came to me carrying a younger sibling. Both children had flies on their faces. It struck me that this little girl could have been my Ella, who had been born into a safe, well-fed environment by virtue of luck alone.

Presto—my magic moment. I knew my purpose. I was done being a tourist. I was going to figure out how children like this little girl could have a chance. A sliver of hope to live a healthy life, free from intestinal worms. That incident convinced me that I first needed to facilitate access to clean water and motivate people to adopt healthy hygiene and sanitation behaviors. I had no idea how steep my learning curve would be and the extent my personal behavior needed to change. My first major obstacle was to slow down my internal clock, to think less, to be more present, and to learn a brand-new set of rules.

## PS #6: RANDOM INCIDENTS OF WONDER AND AWE

- ✦ No ambient light in Tiebele, Burkina Faso, when you sleep on a rooftop. The stars seem close enough to reach out and grab one.

- Tuareg nomads weaving their camels in lazy figure eights to the beat of a haunting melody, accompanied by a flip-flop beating the rhythm on a deflated ball floating in a basin of water in the desert night.
- The village elders of Timia, Niger, exorcized a spirit from a woman who spent the night in the desert and was acting strangely, releasing her stored-up traumatic energy. Another woman danced with the affected woman, twirling and swirling, around and around. Once the dancing women fell to the ground in a trance, the community was assured the evil spirit was gone.
- Lining the main highway in Ghana are zillions of tables with jugs filled with liquid petrol that Nigerians steal from pipelines. The Ghanaians somehow acquire the stolen petrol and sell it by the gallon.
- Small shops on the roadway with blessed names: God Blessed Tires, Praise Jesus Auto Repair, Hallelujah Eats. Great fun and so original. And then there are the T-shirts advertising a loved one's passing: GOD REST THE SOUL OF BIG MAMA or LITTLE BROTHER, RIP.
- I drank the liquid of a coiled snake pickled and preserved in a jar. It freed me from my terror of snakes.
- The effrontery of asking people to change their behavior: These people don't have enough food to eat or safe water to drink, and yet we ask them to trust *us*, complete strangers who have likely never experienced such deprivation, instead of the wisdom of their ancestors' teachings.

## Connection of the Hearts

Susan, a chubby girl growing up in Beverly Hills, California, was a prime target for the neighborhood bullies. She wanted to shrink inside her skin and disappear from her family's privileged upper-middle-class life. Her favorite hiding place was her parents' library, where she immersed herself in the pictures and descriptions of the simple, no-flash-or-glitter lives of Indigenous cultures.

Susan left home as soon as she graduated from high school at seventeen, turning her back on the privileges of the wealthy. She was anxious to get away from her mother and "I deserve everyone's attention" younger sister. She worked her way through a local college instead of attending the high-priced Ivy League school chosen by her parents.

Putting every dollar not needed for food or rent into her *National Geographic* travel fund, Susan hungered to live, even for a short while, inside the compelling pictures she had seen in the magazine. Finally, savings in hand, she found a travel group that specialized in cross-cultural journeys and began her adventures. Susan found she could make heartfelt connections without speaking the same language, whether it be visiting the nuns in Tibet, wheat farmers in Eastern India, or the children at our orphanage in Ethiopia. Some vibrancy inside her woke up, and she was able to leap forward, eager to engage instead of shrinking back. She will never forget the moment one of our little orphan boys sat next to her on the floor, rubbing his arm on hers, curious to see whether the white on her arm would rub off and become as black as his arm.

Susan has never seen herself as better than anyone else. She knows having money and privilege does not make her more deserving. She believes that all people are intrinsically the same—although she admits Indigenous people help her feel greater joy. When her heart is open and she is able to make eye contact, there is a richness in the experience that she doesn't find in the US. Susan suspects we Westerners have become so advanced that we have lost the ability and/or the desire to make heartfelt connections with others.

## AND MY WORLD TURNED

Understanding different people and cultures has expanded my world. I still unconsciously judge people, but not so quickly and not quite as often. Contextual perspective helps me think more creatively and be more innovative. I carry an American passport, but I am a citizen of the world.

# DREAM:
## *Learning from Different People and Cultures*

**D**esire: Broaden my knowledge base by learning from people different from me.

**R**eflect on who I know or how I can meet someone who believes in a different higher power.

**E**xplore where I can interact with someone who is subjected to different prejudices than I am.

**A**cknowledge that feelings and opinions have been influenced by the context of environment.

**M**antra:
Help me embrace diversity,
Discover the strength of others
and the beauty of their being.
Help me not make assumptions
that limit my experience of life.

### WISE WOMAN WORDS

"The more I traveled, the more I realized that
fear makes strangers of people who should be friends."
*–Shirley MacLaine*

# 10

# Defining Your Own "Supposed-Tos"

Picture a suit that covers you from the top of your head to the bottom of your feet. The helmet tells you how to think; the sleeves govern what you do; the gloves determine what you touch; the bodice influences when your stomach clenches and feels queasy; the pants choose how you move; and your shoes pick the path you walk.

This suit of "supposed-tos"—values, beliefs, customs, and traditions—is slipped on us at birth and glued to our bodies as our cognitive awareness develops. Then society takes over, influencing the way we think and behave and determining what we can achieve and attain as members. Laws are social norms formally established at the local, state, or federal level. They carry severe restrictive consequences, including, at times, death. And within any culture, breaking a taboo may cause you to lose your place in society.

These cultural constraints are either prescriptive (people *should* do certain things) or proscriptive (people *should not* do certain things), telling people what they can do and choose, with whom, where, and how they can interact—thereby providing structure and predictability. Primitive societies have basic constraints, ensuring that people know how to obtain food and build shelters. As societies become more complex and science and technology come into play, constraints become more pervasive and invasive.

Social norms particularly govern the behavior of people who share beliefs and practices. Rules dictate religious and spiritual practices, and they empower relationships, childcare, and medical treatment. Everyday aspects of life such as household relationships, dress, grooming, and attitudes are molded to fit these norms, which are transmitted from one generation to the next and play a big role in determining how an individual behaves in any given environment.

That's a lot of baggage to sort through and decide what to keep, what to modify, and what to shed.

## THE ROAD LESS TRAVELED

As children grow up, they learn about social norms and cultural expectations through observation, instruction, and reinforcement from parents, peers, and other social agents. This gives them a sense of who they are and affects how they develop emotionally, socially, and physically.

Countries such as the United States, the United Kingdom, Australia, and New Zealand have individualistic cultures that ascribe great importance to individual goals, self-actualization, autonomy, and uniqueness. Other countries, including China, India, Japan, and South Korea, have largely collectivist cultures, where the individual strives for the benefit and welfare of the social unit rather than focusing on individual needs and achievement.

Social pressure to conform and comply within a culture is intense. In the English language alone, there are more than fifty synonyms for "comply" and forty for "conform." You can adhere to, give in, give up, and obey. You can be compelled, constrained, and forced to yield. You may be coerced to overcome your unwillingness or be threatened by violence. Arguments like "It's for the good of the community" and "Everyone agrees that you should" are used to make you feel obligated.

I accept that rules are necessary to create a sense of regularity, predictability, and subjective inevitability. We do not want to plunge into a haphazard, chaotic, uncontrollable world. However, I am against mind control, programming of beliefs, and silos of class opportunity. I chafe at allowing some "all-knowing body" to channel my life along the grains of conformity, à la religious dictums. I accept that life is not fair but firmly believe that everyone has the same innate value as a human being.

The idea of someone dictating my thoughts, words, and actions has always made my body itch and my head ache. I was not okay with my family's beliefs and determined that I would decide the "rules" to govern my life.

I admit that the path I took to shed cultural constraints was radical and not a road easily traveled. Crazy as it sounds, it was easier for me to flee to Africa than to stand up to Steve. I was eager to fight for the rights of others, but my confidence to self-advocate was stalled at the toddler stage: Stand up. One step forward. Fall. Cry (internally). Crawl forward.

I left my big house overlooking Puget Sound in February 2008, carrying a bag full of technology: computer, video camera, still camera, Polaroid camera, tape recorder, and all kinds of chargers, including a solar panel. Another duffel bag was full of gifts for interviewees, Ziploc bags of incidentals to keep me healthy, and a few clothes. I was off to spend forty days in Ethiopia. Little did I know it would be forty days of eating spaghetti!

Travel tip: You can actually eat spaghetti every night for forty days and lose weight if you live and work in the bush in equatorial Africa.

I sat in the SeaTac airport gate that afternoon, primed for a solo adventure, with no one controlling me. Giddy. Nervous. Determined.

### WHY AFRICA? WHY NOW?

After my epiphany with that young girl in the Sahara Desert and before I started my own NGO, I started researching nonprofit organizations working in sub-Saharan Africa. I was referred to a small NGO that worked in Niger, Mali, and Ethiopia. I instantly connected with the founder and, in January 2007, visited her in Arizona. She had structured her life around her passion, decorated her house, and spent her evenings how *she* wanted. I envied her freedom of choice.

She was trying to grow her organization's capacity, and although I had no experience in donor development, I agreed to create a strategy to increase her funding, and she would share what she had learned about implementing programs in Africa.

Her major fundraising activity was running medical missions staffed by volunteers and local doctors who provided mobile clinics in the bush. I joined the July 2007 trip to South Omo Valley to conduct an in-depth analysis of the program. After traveling for two days over potholed single-lane roads, competing for the right-of-way with trucks, goats, cows, donkeys, and pedestrians, we arrived in the valley, the home of eight tribes. The population in 2007 was estimated at 200,000 people. Estimates fifteen years later are closer to 750,000, due to the influx of refugees from South Sudan.

The people of South Omo are extremely poor, malnourished, starving, and sick. Traditionally, these tribes are pastoralists (seminomadic), raising cattle and goats for their livelihood. Living for centuries in a dry area with high temperature, they have followed their livestock in search of grazing grounds and water during the dry season. Now, with climate change and diminishing resources (the government grabbed huge blocks of land along the Weyto and Omo Rivers to lure foreign investment), the tribes have been forced to settle, miles away from water, and attempt to survive on sorghum and maize planted in rocky, infertile soil.

The lifestyle they learned from their ancestors is no longer viable. Historically, South Omo tribes were collegial and collaborative. Now they are fierce enemies, fighting over resources. The arrival of refugees from South Sudan has exacerbated the tension.

This medical mission opened my eyes and altered my place in the world. We camped in three different tribal areas: Mursi (known for large lip and ear plates), Kara (recognized by body piercings), and Hamar (where women's hair is twisted into ringlets, dripping ocher-colored mud, nonremovable iron choker collars are forged around their necks, and they are clothed in yokes made of goatskin).

*Me with two little buddies*

The days started early and ended late. During those eight days, we saw more than 1,800 people who didn't feel well and demanded medicine—any pill would do. There was no time to evaluate, assess, and treat. All five of us volunteers quickly became dispirited. The need was so great, and our ability to serve was grossly inadequate. It's easy to say, "This doesn't work, but we tried to help." The more challenging question is "How could you help these people have a chance for a healthy life?"

The Hamar tribe captured my heart. The population was estimated at 45,000 people living in fifteen kebeles (the smallest government-designated entity). I decided to select three of the twelve kebeles assigned to the Turmi Health Center and figured the most efficient way to make decisions was to conduct a survey. I needed to identify what initiatives to implement and which communities would be most receptive before applying for grants.

I was a bored woman ready to escape an unsatisfying marriage who wanted to feel fulfilled. I had no idea what success looked like, but I was an entrepreneur and would figure it out. The Hamar people's powerlessness and suffering deeply touched me, and there was no turning back. After all, they were people just like me. Helping them became my purpose.

Numerous aid organizations were implementing programs in South Omo, and some had significant impact, while others not so much. I set out to thoroughly understand the overall need and identify what inputs (wells, schools, income-generating activities, health initiatives, etc.) were necessary for change to be sustainable. How do you make a positive difference that sticks in a culture that is bound up in ancient sanctions, social norms, and taboos?

Hamar customs and behaviors are firmly rooted in tradition: "Our ancestors did this, and they lived. Our only chance to survive is to do what they did." Unfortunately, the environment has changed dramatically with the aforementioned government-imposed boundaries, land grabs, and climate change. The people are starving without access to grazing grounds and water, so their livelihood is disappearing. They can't read or write, have no reliable source of outside information, and don't feel safe. They aren't safe. South Omo, sharing borders with Kenya and South Sudan, is rife with gunrunning.

## BABOONS MAY BE BETTER OFF

The plight of the Hamar women and children tugged at my heart. Little girls start carrying loads of grain equal to their body weight when they are five years old, walking for miles on sandy ground covered with rocks and stones, thorns, and bristles. They begin the arduous task of grinding grain when they are seven and are married to elders as soon as their menses begins. The births of female babies are celebrated for three reasons: They do the work, they produce more babies who do more work, and their bride price brings wealth to the family (goats, sheep, cows, and guns with ammunition). They have a name, but it is seldom used. My friend Ama Oita confided, "We are treated worse than the baboon in the bush."

### *Never Alone*

As soon as a Hamar girl is married, she lives in her husband's compound. Each wife has her own tukul, a round hut made of acacia branches. The opening is about one square foot, a foot above the ground. (Try climbing through that as a sixty-year-old with a knee replacement). A tukul's diameter is approximately ten feet and provides shelter for the wife, her children, her baby goats, and her lambs. A compound often has five to six tukuls, depending on the number of wives. The elder makes his rounds according to his whim of the day.

Few young men get to marry because elders own the livestock used for bride price. This creates a real problem for adrenaline-charged young men who spend many lonely days and nights following the family's livestock, far from the watchful eyes of their fathers. Rape runs rampant.

## GULU BOLA'S SUPPOSED-TOS

1. *Be the donkey.*

Throughout sub-Saharan Africa, small donkeys carry water, sacks of grain, and bundles of sticks and branches. Not in Hamar country, where there is an ample supply of large Abyssinian donkeys; there, the women carry all loads. Men carry their berkota (a small wooden headrest that doubles as a tiny stool). Donkeys roam freely and graze.

One day, we were asked to transport fifty kilograms of sorghum to our camp for an elder. We did. Several hours later, he showed up with his daughter, about ten years old and weighing less than sixty pounds. He separated the sorghum into two equal sacks, making sure hers was twenty-five kilos, or sixty pounds. When I protested, he laughed and said it was good training for her. Once the little girl's sack was strapped on her back, another man showed up and took the father's share. The father walked off carrying nothing. Grrr.

Young Hamar girls, soon to be married.

2. *Have lots of babies.*

It is common for a Hamar elder (a male who owns property and livestock) to father twelve to twenty-plus children. When the first wife stops reproducing, he marries another, younger woman. The elder wants more male children to follow the livestock and more female children to carry loads and provide him with her bride-price (more livestock and guns).

Owning cattle is the only way for a young man to acquire a wife.

It's an essential, nonnegotiable part of the bride price. But shrinking pasture lands and limited access to water is exacerbating the death of cattle. Young men, armed with guns from gunrunning, are angry, frustrated, and disenfranchised.

As I mentioned earlier, Gulu was born into a family of seven children: four boys and three girls. Before she reached her menses, her parents had already started negotiating with the father of a young man who had "jumped the bulls"—his *ecooli*, an ancient ritual to prove that the young man had attained manhood.

An ecooli ceremony is a family's biggest event. Distant clansmen, relatives, and friends walk days to attend. The lucky young man spends the day strutting around naked, blowing a horn fashioned from a bull, feasting, and drinking beer made of sorghum and honey. Meanwhile, the young man's friends whip the bare backs of his sisters and female relatives with pliable whippet branches. The whipping leaves deep wounds, prominent scars for life.

A female is *supposed to* be whipped to prove her love for her brother or cousin. By submitting to the ritual, the girls show their devotion to family, and they also provide a bit of an insurance policy, as their suffering creates an obligation. During hard times, the young man will care for the young women who can show proof of their sacrifice for him.

After much to-do, five or six bulls are herded together, head to tail, in a column. The young man jumps on the back of the first bull, skips over the backs of the remaining bulls held tightly together, jumps off the last bull, turns around, and jumps up and repeats the process four times. When he jumps down the last time, he's a man, ready to marry and make babies.

Ecooli is very controversial. It has become the number one tourist attraction and generates "cash to watch" for the hosting family (and tourism agent) but is classified as a "harmful traditional practice," which means dollars are being invested to stop it because of the whipping of the girls. A terrible side effect of the whipping is the accelerated spread of HIV/AIDS. Hamar girls are frequently raped and infected by truck drivers traveling through Turmi. During ecooli, the same butter poultice is used on all the girls' backs, so the disease spreads to her extended family.

After Gulu's "chosen" husband jumped the bulls, several of his friends came to her father's tukul to collect her. That evening, Gulu and her closest friends sat close together on the ground, singing and clapping, crooning, "Ee aah, ee aah" (You go, you go) very sadly.

Gulu would leave in the morning to live with her new husband's mother for four months to learn how to care for him properly, and an iron collar would be forged around her neck. The new couple would not have relations during that time to prove that Gulu was not spoiled goods.

Gulu's new hut was in Minogelti, one of the most dangerous Hamar kebeles. There is no "town center," no services, just a police outpost. It is very remote (thirty-two miles from the nearest health center) and shares a long border with the Dassanech tribe. Whenever one of the scarce wells is working in either of the two kebeles, young men hide and wait to accost the young girls of the opposing tribe when they come to collect water.

Even in tribes whose basic needs are not met and a high percentage of people are stunted, outliers occur. Gulu is definitely an outlier. Her cognitive skills are remarkable. Although the elders (male) are the decision-makers, Gulu's innate curiosity coupled with high intelligence caused her natural leadership skills and creativity to be noticed in a community struggling to survive. Over time, she took on the role as advocate for the community and tried to entice NGOs to work in Minogelti.

Gulu followed the norms of her society and had eight children, six boys and two girls. She understood that a woman's value is determined by the number of live babies born. But as soon as her husband married a second wife, she decided to leave him. She was done suffering his cruel and abusive behavior. Her decision to leave carried an exorbitant price.

3. *Have no rights.*

Hamar women are not allowed to inherit anything—no land, no livestock, no form of livelihood. They are not allowed to divorce. The husband can keep marrying new wives, but since a wife is "purchased," she is the property of her husband, and it is taboo to leave her marriage.

When Gulu left, she was ostracized.

Ostracism, one of the cruelest social punishments known to man, is a slow death sentence in Hamar. No one was allowed to communicate with Gulu or give her shelter or food. She was beaten and isolated. Her husband demanded that she be killed if she didn't leave the area. Gulu hid out while the community raged among themselves.

The elders deliberated for days. Her husband's supporters banded together, spreading falsehoods and ranting, "Kill her, kill her." However, over the years, Gulu had become her community's most effective advocate, and the elders depended on her. At the last moment, influential elders intuited what would happen to Minogelti should Gulu's voice be silenced. Gulu received word in her hideout that her death sentence had been rescinded; she could live. Her husband was told to be satisfied with his second wife. The community defied tradition and chose Gulu, their voice. Eventually, she built and lived in her own hut in Minogelti.

Gulu continues to be the architect of her life. She got rid of the iron yoke around her neck the day her eldest child married. She encouraged her kids to chart their courses: one is the kebele manager (Minogelti's mayor), one is a teacher, two are students, two are shepherds, one helps in the community, and one is deceased. She has twelve grandchildren: six girls and six boys. All will learn to read, write, and speak Amharic (Gulu goes to the UN, chapter 12).

4. *Be normal at birth.*

In Hamar, follow the norms at birth (despite your inability to control any of the following) or you die:

- Norm 1: Do not be born to a single mother.
- Norm 2: Do not be born less than twelve moons (one year) after your parents are married.
- Norm 3: Make sure your bottom-jaw teeth come in before your top teeth.
- Norm 4: Make sure you do not lose your lower-jaw teeth by accident.
- Norm 5: If you are a twin, make sure you and your sibling are not firstborn.

If any of these norms are violated, you will be declared a *mingi* and ostracized before you are two years old. You will be left out in a field to either starve to death or be eaten by wild animals. You are considered bad luck for the tribe. If you are not killed, the rains will not come, the cattle will die, there will be no food, and neighboring tribes will attack. If your parents do not abandon you, they will be killed or ostracized. It has been estimated that more than 100 children are abandoned to die each year in Hamar.

When we agreed to implement an orphans and vulnerable children program to intervene and care for, support, and reunify mingi children with birth families, we wanted to build the facility in our main project area, Wonga Bayno. The elders were terrified that terrible things would happen to them. Time for hardball. "Let us build the facility, or we construct wells and build schools elsewhere." They agreed, and wonder of all wonders, the community and the kids prospered.

Gulu and her friends helped me gain perspective. Yes, others had defined my supposed-tos, but I am a well-educated White woman with enough resources to support myself. I have access to the internet, good health, mobility, a wealth of experience, and I am surrounded by professionals. I am *not powerless*. It was time for me to get over my past and focus on the needs of others. Turn the page and start a new chapter.

My theme song became "Star Girls," by Leandra Peak and Neal Hagberg. Give it a listen if you want to be inspired.

## TO CLAP OR NOT TO CLAP

How do you develop the moxie and conviction to take charge of the trajectory of your life without escaping to Africa or its equivalent? I admit my path was a tad extreme!

Consider the question "To clap or not to clap?" asked by Shelley Row in her article "Four Steps to Loosen the Grip of 'Supposed-Tos.'"[22] Do you feel compelled to clap along with everyone else after experiencing a subpar performance? It would feel awkward not to clap. It's a supposed-to, the social norm. Clapping doesn't make us right or wrong; it makes us socially comfortable. We do what everyone else does. We clap.

Defining our own supposed-tos takes conscious decision-making, courage to swim upstream, and a willingness to feel awkward and uncomfortable.

Shelley Row suggests these steps to help loosen the grip of supposed-tos:

1. *Recognize the Rule.*

When you sense a churning in your gut as you internally debate *Should I or shouldn't I do this or that*, notice it. The nagging feeling signals discomfort. There's a supposed-to, a rule, in play that perhaps needs examining.

2. *Recognize the Source of the Rule.*

Supposed-tos may have come from our family's belief system, our communities, or our religious book of truth (Bible, Torah, *Bhagavata Purana*, Tipitaka, Qur'an). Perhaps we absorbed unspoken rules from

---

22   Shelley Row, "Four Steps to Loosen the Grip of 'Supposed-Tos,'" Blue Fjord Leaders, November 6, 2014, https://www.bluefjordleaders.com/break-the-power-of-your-supposed-tos-with-these-four-steps-to-clap-or-not-to-clap-that-is-the-question/.

manipulated feelings—*I should live near my parents and have kids*—or from watching TV or perusing social media posts.

Think about it, reflect, and explore. Understanding the source of the rule makes it easier to release the control it has on our thoughts and behavior.

3. *Supposed-tos Are Optional.*

All those old rules—cultural constraints, social norms, taboos—are optional if they don't sync with who we are now. They might currently govern us, consciously or subconsciously, but we can intentionally *choose* what to believe and how to behave.

A word of caution from Albert Einstein: "Just because you don't believe in something doesn't mean it isn't true." Or as author Robert Fulghum said, "Don't believe everything you think."

4. *Write a New Rule.*

Take the old rule and rewrite it to fit your values and situation today. Let your thinking evolve with your exposure and experiences. We are never too old to shed current beliefs and adopt new norms. After all, our personalities become more complex, layered, and nuanced as we migrate from one place to another.

An article from *Psychology Today* about resisting social pressure provides helpful advice on how to gain ownership of your supposed-tos.[23]

5. *The Illusion of Others.*

Pleasing others is a moving target. Social pressures influence expectations. They are *not* reality. When others get frustrated because we don't behave as they expect or satisfy their needs, that's *their* expectation, not *our* mandate. Likewise, we don't have the right to prescribe how others should behave. The way I live my life is my

---

[23] Gustavo Razzetti, "Live Your Life for You, Not to Please Expectations," *Psychology Today,* October 24, 2018, https://www.psychologytoday.com/us/blog/the-adaptive-mind/201810/live-your-life-you-not-please-expectations.

choice, and your actions and beliefs are yours.

As Jodi Picoult so aptly says in her novel *Nineteen Minutes*, "There are two ways to be happy: improve your reality or lower your expectations."

6. *Put Your Oxygen Mask on First.*

Accepting ourselves fully, flaws included, is the foundation for a long-term friendship with ourselves. When we accept who we are, we take charge of our supposed-tos. Research by Kristin Neff shows that compassionate acts we do for ourselves release "feel-good" hormones.[24] Increased levels of oxytocin make us feel comforted, calm, and connected.

## Principles Versus the Principal

Robin Gabbert, a polite, straight-A student who sang and played the guitar, was cruising through school in a small town in the Deep South. It was the early seventies, and girls could finally wear jeans, bell bottoms and peasant blouses, peace signs on rawhide strings, hoop earrings, and suede fringe jackets. No more dresses, girdles, and uncomfortable shoes. Boys were growing their hair Beatles style or longer. Life was good until Dr. Hardly, the new high school principal from the Dark Ages, arrived during Robin's junior year.

Dr. Hardly mandated that girls only wear skirts and dresses no more than three inches above the knees, pants and jeans were not allowed, and boys' hair must be cut neatly above their ears. Grumbling, girls dragged out

---

24  Research by Kristin Neff referenced in Gustavo Razzetti, "Live Your Life for You, Not to Please Expectations" *Psychology Today, October 24, 2018*, https://www.psychologytoday.com/us/blog/the-adaptive-mind/201810/live-your-life-for-you-not-to-please-expectations.

their discards, and boys snipped their hair. Some parents and teachers disagreed with the Hardly mandate, but no one publicly opposed him. (After all, he had a PhD and had been hired to raise college admittance scores.) No one, that is, except for Robin, the editor of the *Hogg's Breath* student newspaper. Her editorial did not specifically name the principal but did criticize his policy and made an unflattering analogy between his desert boots and gestapo boots. As soon as Mrs. Pinchy, the teacher supervisor of the *Hogg's Breath*, got wind of the editorial, "One Step Forward, Two Goose Steps Backward," Robin was marched into Dr. Hardly's office.

Mrs. Pinchy and Dr. Hardly glared at her. She glared back. Eventually Mrs. Pinchy made her pitch: "Robin, now that you've written your little diatribe, gotten this off of your chest, I'm sure you know that this kind of article is inappropriate for a high school newspaper? Withdraw it."

Robin refused. She argued that high school students should be allowed the right of free speech and freedom of expression. So a fuming Dr. Hardly quashed the editorial; it was never printed. But Dr. Hardly was not done with this defiant girl who dared to insinuate that he was a Nazi. He managed to block Robin from graduating with her class on a technicality even though she was the only local student to have scored in the top 2 percent of the state in standardized testing.

Refusing to let Dr. Hardly's actions define her, Robin went on to college and law school, graduating third in her class and eventually became a "super lawyer" in her field of practice.

Now retired, Robin has found her true love—poetry—and has since savored a new way of expressing herself about issues ranging from politics and art to grief and abuse. Her specialty is ekphrastic poetry, or writing poetry in conversation with art. It turns out this wise woman has both left- and right-brain abilities.

## THE MAGIC OF NO

It becomes possible to say no once we internalize that expectations do not define reality. Not easy, but possible. Feeling uncomfortable is distasteful. The fear of feeling unacceptable is worse.

I had to rejigger my supposed-tos to align with reality before I could feel a sense of self-love by saying no.

When my intuitive daughter Shay asked me pointedly why I was still married to Steve, I hemmed and hawed and finally confessed I didn't have the energy to deal with divorce. Shay gave me the courage to sever the ties when she said she would help me. I came to realize that my marriage to Steve was based on fear, not hope—fear of being alone, fear of not being important to someone, and fear of not being socially acceptable. Overcoming those fears set me free. The constraints of being his wife were gone. Woohoo!

When I left Ethiopia, my supposed-tos included moving back to Minnesota to live near my kids and grandkids—doing grandma things like baking cookies, babysitting, and making family dinners.

Truth be told, I was tired. Empty. I had nothing more to give. All my energy had been used up. I needed time to reflect and refresh. Trying to live that supposed-to life would have been misery for me and my kids.

Many years later, in 2023, Bill and I moved to Northern California immediately after I had major surgery. Too much too fast for a seventy-four-year-old. My concerned daughters pleaded to come out and help me settle our house. Fortunately, I had a moment of clarity. They can't cook, and they don't clean and don't eat the same food we do. All of us would have been frustrated by unrealistic expectations. The most loving response to their plea was to say no.

Learning to accept reality is hard but necessary. Removing or lowering your expectation bar releases unrealistic pressure. It allows you to give your best.

You are *you*—a divine being with your own moral compass to calibrate. No one has the right to determine whether you are good or bad, acceptable or discard material, a sinner or a saint. You are the boss of you. Free your soul and let it soar.

Be curious. Learn from your mistakes. Collect information. Reflect. Explore. Be the navigator of your own course.

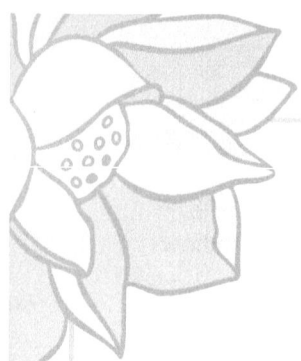

# DREAM:
## *Defining My Supposed-tos*

**D**esire: Choose the values and beliefs that guide my thoughts, words, and actions.

**R**eflect on the values I want to define me as a person.

**E**xplore my familial and/or social beliefs that don't feel quite right.

**A**cknowledge that my actions and words communicate my values.

**M**antra:
Like the running river, my being flows.
My spirit soars on the wings of my fancy.
Bonds loosen, shackles tumble down.
I become free to be me.

### WISE WOMAN WORDS

*"I distrust those people who know so well
what God wants them to do, because I notice
it always coincides with their own desires."*
—Susan B. Anthony

# 11

# Activating Empathy and Compassion

Wouldn't it be great if you could flip a switch when you become overwhelmed by stressful situations or people's negative energy? Instead of being sucked into the muck, you would rise above and calmly navigate the unpleasantness.

It's possible to develop a serenity switch. Our emotions are not set in stone. Create a strategy, and with intentional practice you can alter the way you react to challenging situations.

Empathy is the ability to understand the feelings of others and even share their pain while remaining aware that it's someone else's emotion. Empathy acknowledges that no one is alone. This mode of relating can lead to a giving, joyful state of being. Compassion converts empathetic understanding into action. Fortunately, living a compassionate life can be learned.

Sara Konrath, PhD, an associate professor of social psychology at Indiana University, believes that the form of empathy most beneficial for the giver *and* the receiver is an "other-oriented response." "It's a cognitive style of perspective taking," she says, "where someone imagines another person's perspective, reads their emotions, and can understand them in general."[25]

---

[25] Ashley Abramson, "Cultivating empathy," American Psychological Association, November 1, 2021, https://www.apa.org/monitor/2021/11/feature-cultivating-empathy.

Hillary Clinton, in a 2014 speech at Georgetown University, stressed the importance of "showing respect even for one's enemies, trying to understand, and insofar as is psychologically possible, empathize with their perspective and point of view."[26] Empathizing does not mean we agree, but it allows us to understand another's current actions and predict future actions.

## SEETHING VESUVIUS

My desire to comprehend the atrocities and deprivations shown on television in 1994 started my journey. I intellectually understood that terrible things were happening to people through no fault of their own, but I couldn't begin to imagine how one dealt with suddenly being forced to leave home and flee for one's life. I knew that in order to relate, I needed to understand the victims' stories, perspectives, and environment. I made the conscious choice to stimulate empathy. As Dr. Yvette Erasmus says, "Empathy is a choice-based action fueled by your heart."[27]

It took me years to understand the perspective of an urban Ethiopian or tribal elder living in South Omo. Seeing the exploitation of women and experiencing the corruption, lying, and manipulation by those with even the slightest advantage over the person next to them made me seethe with anger. Negative emotions simmered in my being, creating a roadblock. I desperately wanted to be an endless source of peace, love, and harmony, but that was impossible when my system was clogged. I could facilitate compassionate action, but until I was able to convert negative emotion into positive energy, a constant battle churned within me.

---

26 Sara Konrath, "What's the Matter with Empathy?" January 24, 2017, *Greater Good Magazine, https://greatergood.berkeley.edu/article/item/whats_the_matter_with_empathy.*

27 Dr. Yvette Erasmus, "Is it Empathy, or Enabling?" Medium, Jul 14, 2019, https://dryvetteerasmus.medium.com/is-it-empathy-or-enabling-fb625b477448.

## RELENTLESS NOISE

The noise of Addis isn't background noise. It's in-your-face, headache-producing clamor 100 percent of the time. The windows of my house did not close tightly, with gaps everywhere in the windows, doors, frames—you name it. It seemed like people talked twenty-four hours a day. Nonstop loudspeakers blasted preaching by Orthodox priests. Through my windows I heard goats bleating, chickens squawking, radios blaring, and donkeys braying. It was so noisy that if I wanted to watch a movie on my computer, I had to hold it inches from my ear to hear it. I struggled to find calm.

My least favorite Ethiopian Orthodox ceremony was Timkit, the celebration of Epiphany. One year, five churches set up loudspeakers in a large field a block from my house. Ceaseless sermons blasted out of competing speakers for forty-two hours straight. It was a loud, discordant whirlwind of noise. Eventually it dawned on me that instead of seething with resentment, I should use the opportunity to practice my mantra. I failed miserably. I didn't feel a speck of peace, love, or harmony. I was going insane from all the preaching and screeching.

There's a saying on a mug: "Peace is finding tranquility in the midst of chaos." I had to find a variable I could change. Aha! Rent a different house.

My friend Delphine found an island of tranquility for me, hidden behind a blue gate. A modest house with its own flower and vegetable garden gave me a sliver of separation and seclusion. I started to appreciate waking up to the sounds of a new day—listening to the town crier announce the events of the night in a singsong voice and to the Adhan, the Islamic call to prayer by the muezzin. As the sun rose, the short transition between night and day was heralded by a symphony of birds. I ate my oatmeal on the back stoop, enjoying the songs of the mourning doves. A time of peace before opening my gate and stepping into the madness of the day.

### CONGRUENCE IN FEAR

By and large, Ethiopian people are loving, kind, caring, and eager to help, but they are surrounded by an environment of fear. Fear of neighbors reporting antigovernment views. Fear of not having enough food to eat. Fear of violence. Fear of getting cholera from the drinking water. Fear of not being paid. Fear of anything and everything bad happening to them.

In my experience, this overwhelming fear could cause myopic, self-absorbed behavior in employees. It was difficult to get people to accept any type of delayed gratification. Personal benefits needed to be realized immediately, even when the funding was not in place. Managers often said yes while thinking, *That will never happen.*

My management skills, developed in a hope-based business environment, required drastic modification in this "Once you are hired you cannot be fired" world. Frustrated, angry, and impatient, I was initially unable to embrace the joy of finding my life's purpose.

### ENERGY INVERTER REQUIRED

In South Omo, when we installed solar panels in our base camp a million miles from nowhere, we used an inverter, which converted direct current (DC) electricity from our solar panels to alternating current (AC) electricity to power our lights and computers.

That's what I needed: a human energy inverter.

Rudyard Kipling's words from his poem "We and They"—"All the people like us are We, and everyone else is They"—describe the bottleneck preventing many people from activating empathy and compassion. To convert the me-versus-them into "us," we need to understand the other person's environment (reality), their perspective (view), and their innate potential (the cards they were dealt). Like a lump of coal under pressure, negative energy can become a positive force. We just need to find and then leverage the right pressure points.

## UNDERSTAND THE ENVIRONMENT AND THE REALITY OF OTHERS

Eventually, I came to understand that the behavior I found frustrating in Ethiopia was necessary for its people to survive in that environment. The all-powerful government was suspicious of its citizens. Neighbors were suspicious of neighbors. Employees were suspicious of managers, who were suspicious of their bosses.

Life was congruent if you were afraid: Be nice. Be careful what you say. Pretend to agree. Be vigilant.

In the field, it was a different story. Tribal members depended on each other. When an old widow lacked food, the clan elder made sure she received what she needed. They cared. They shared. They lived and died together.

There were four widespread clusters of compounds in Wonga Bayno kebele, our primary project area. Kasha, the most difficult to access, was in dire need of water. There was no road, so we had to hike to Kasha to determine where to construct water schemes. About thirty minutes into a hot, hilly, four-hour walk, we met two women running up the narrow trail. They had heard I was in Wonga Bayno, and their sister was in desperate need of help. A month before, she had given birth, and now her stomach was hard, and she was vomiting. We agreed to take her to the Turmi Health Center, but first they needed to transport her by litter to our vehicle.

The walk was arduous. We came upon the ailing woman surrounded by ten community members busily constructing the litter to carry her to our car. When I touched the woman, I felt her body rattle. We quickly hurried to fetch our vehicle to move it to the nearest possible meeting point.

As soon as the litter party came into view, Bali, the head elder of Wonga Bayno, jumped out and ran toward them. Our community worker, Emanny, and I trailed behind.

Suddenly, a young man we later discovered was the sick woman's brother came running at me, pointing his AK-47, aiming to shoot. One man grabbed him from behind to wrestle away the gun while Bali jumped in front of him and dismantled the magazine.

The woman had just died, and her brother was crazed with grief. Bali yelled for me to turn around immediately and leave. No argument from me. My companions and I ducked and fled.

Once I could breathe again, I was overwhelmed by the compassion of the community. There was immediate cooperation to make the litter and carry it for hours over difficult terrain. There was no hesitation from Bali in putting himself in danger to save me from being shot. The community's instinctive reaction was kindness in action.

The Hamar exemplify what Jeffrey D. Sachs calls the poverty trap in his book *The End of Poverty*:

> Consider the kind of poverty caused by a lack of capital per person. Poor rural villages lack trucks, paved roads, power generators, irrigation channels. Human capital is very low, with hungry, disease-ridden, and illiterate villagers struggling for survival. Natural capital is depleted: the trees have been cut down and soil nutrients exhausted. The need is for more capital—physical, human, natural—that requires more saving . . . but when [people] are utterly destitute, they need their entire income, or more, just to survive. There is no margin of income above survival that can be invested for the future.[28]

---

28   Jeffrey D. Sachs, *The End of Poverty* (Penguin Books, 2006).

## UNDERSTAND "THEIR" PERSPECTIVE

Earlier, I shared the plight of Hamar women, valued for the work they did and the number of babies they birthed. Eventually, I understood the plight of the Hamar elders. They did not have the tools, skills, or cognitive ability (particularly when it came to imagining, learning words, and using language) necessary to survive and thrive in today's world.

One day, when we returned to camp, ten agitated elders were waiting for us. The leader held out a dirty, wrinkled sheet of paper that he wanted translated. It was a letter to the government, asking permission to graze their cattle on government land because drought had turned Hamar grazing lands to dust.

The elders, who spoke only the Hamar language, had asked a distant relative with a first-grade education to write the letter for them, but they didn't trust that the letter said what they wanted. These proud men, who were responsible for the survival of 3,000 people, had to rely on outsiders to convey their most important request of the year.

As a result of my survey of the Hamar kebeles, we pondered the viability of implementing initiatives to support the alternative basic education schools scattered about the rural areas. We discovered that few elders allowed their children (boys) to attend because education was not valued. Many felt that if their boys were educated, they would move to Turmi and would no longer be willing to follow the livestock or plow fields by hand. Ninety-five percent of the Hamar males surveyed stated that if a girl were educated, her value would decrease. She would not command an adequate bride price. Once we understood the Hamar elders' perspective, we set out to alter their view. We tied learning to earning.

Our original plan was to empower women by teaching them simple arithmetic and basic Amharic phrases so the women's cooperative could earn money. The men liked the idea, but when learning time encroached on working time, it became problematic. We needed to provide more immediate gratification. Men made the decisions, and they needed to receive direct benefit to learn the value of education.

We scrambled to cobble together funding from disparate donors (Boeing, twenty-two Rotary clubs, individuals) to develop a targeted curriculum and hire teachers. We used a "carrot and stick" approach. The carrot was to receive food or a source of income. The stick was the requirement that the person receiving the carrot had to attend school.

Soon, families had home gardens, some became chicken farmers, and more than 500 tribal members became paid community teachers. Opportunities to earn money were predicated on actively participating in healthy hygiene and sanitation behaviors and learning new skills. It was a simple equation and easy to understand. Father/husband wants money to purchase grain? Then daughter/wife attends school.

An unexpected victory occurred when men and women learning together and practicing joint problem-solving created an "aha!" moment for the men. They were surprised to learn that the women actually had some good ideas! We had accidentally stumbled on a way to start shifting cultural norms in favor of gender equality.

### UNDERSTAND "THEIR" ABILITY TO PROCESS

Ethiopians, like many others born in poor, undeveloped countries, often have a fundamental "bad card in the deck" dilemma to overcome.

In America, most pregnant mothers receive vitamins and specific nutritional advice from the time they become pregnant and up to a year after giving birth. As we know, proper nutrition enables healthy cognitive development. In contrast, when I started working in Ethiopia, more than 67 percent of the adults suffered from stunting as a child. This represented more than 26.1 million people of working age who were not able to achieve their potential due to child undernutrition. Stunted children fall sick more often. They miss opportunities to learn, perform less well in school, and grow up economically disadvantaged, which means they are more likely to suffer from chronic diseases.

Fortunately, thanks to USAID and other development agencies,

Ethiopia has made some progress toward achieving the target for stunting, but 36.8 percent of children under five years of age are still affected.

## WIIFM: EMPATHY AND COMPASSION

During my JobBOSS days, various managers took turns leading team-building exercises. One Friday, our customer service manager facilitated the "survival of the Visigoth." I was paired with Karen, a well-respected customer service rep, and was handed a description of the needs of Visigoth #1. Karen received the same for Visigoth #2. The purpose of the exercise was to make sure your Visigoth survived. My argument for Visigoth #1 was aggressive. Karen shrank back in her chair, obviously afraid to contradict me. She gave in, and I got what my Visigoth needed while her Visigoth got nothing.

When the facilitator asked who was able to save their Visigoth, I proudly raised my hand. A few minutes later, my pride turned to shame. I was appalled to learn that while Visigoth #1 needed the fruit of a certain gourd, Visigoth #2 only needed the rind of the gourd to survive. If I had asked Karen what her needs were before aggressively going after my Visigoth's needs, both could have survived. Fortunately, several of my employees were better team players than I was.

Practicing empathy from another person's perspective changed the dynamics of my relationship with my daughter Melissa. She was the oldest child in the family for the first eleven years of her life. When I married Steve, his daughter, Jana, took Melissa's place as the oldest, and Steve took her place as my confidante. Melissa even lost the privacy of her own bedroom. Jana got her own room, while Melissa had to share with Leah, Steve's youngest daughter.

My marriage and our attempt to blend families had a debilitating effect on Melissa. She felt disenfranchised and became angry and resentful. My daughter Shay, on the other hand, was a compliant "don't make waves" type of kid. Melissa demanded attention. David, the baby, needed attention. Shay was often ignored.

There is no do-over card, but I'm lucky that my kids have forgiven me, and during the last twenty-plus years, we have learned new behaviors together.

When Melissa became a mother, she fiercely loved her daughter, Ella, and worked to protect her from me. Meanwhile, I was convinced that I was now a good role model for Ella and wanted to be with her as much as possible. Melissa was in control until Ella turned eighteen, and I strove to understand and respect Melissa's perspective. Fortunately, our deep love for each other, and for Ella, has helped us work through these issues. Not easy, and painful at times, but joy really does come in the morning.

Raymond Mar, PhD, a professor of psychology at York University in Toronto, studies how reading fiction and other kinds of character-driven stories can help people better understand others and the world. "To understand stories, we have to understand characters, their motivations, interactions, reactions, and goals," he says. "It's possible that while understanding stories, we can improve our ability to understand real people in the real world at the same time."[29]

Compassion has been described as having a radiating effect, spreading kindness and forgiveness to others, even those who have treated us badly. Compassion has the potential to neutralize a desire for aggression, punishment, or revenge. Mindfulness, developed through meditation, can function as empathy training.

When I was packing my belongings after my divorce from Steve, thoughts of blame and resentment for his attitude toward my kids kept running through my mind. I practiced slamming it down with a healthy dose of chanting, "Peace, love, harmony."

Filling my mind with positive, affirming thoughts stopped my downward spiral. Months after the divorce, I was able to understand and empathize with how he behaved. I didn't like it and didn't condone it, but the negative force lost its power over me.

---

29   Ashley Abramson, "Cultivating empathy."

## WHO IS CIVILIZED?

According to *Merriam-Webster*, being civilized is characterized by taste, refinement, or restraint. The thesaurus lists synonyms such as "cultured," "educated," "refined," "enlightened," "polite," "elegant," "sophisticated," and "urbane." The antonyms of civilized include "wild" and "barbarous" (also "cruel," "brutal," "vicious," "ferocious," "fierce").

My friends, members of the Dassanech and Hamar ethnic groups, are not formally educated. They often forage for nuts to eat. They wear goatskin (Hamar women) or are bare-breasted (Dassanech women). Their cultural ceremonies include running naked across the backs of bulls (Hamar men) and female circumcision (Dassanech), and they have never visited art galleries or listened to a symphony. If lucky, their shoes are made from worn-out tires.

On most days, Westerners shower. We dress in clean clothes. We can read, write, discuss ideas, and make long-range, complicated plans. Although too many people in the West still struggle to make ends meet, most have access to social assistance programs and safety nets.

In South Omo, tribes must rely on each other. They kill each other over access to water and grazing grounds to survive, but they also help each other to live.

One Friday in Addis, while waiting for a taxi on the side of a busy street, I noticed three people fighting each other about fifty feet up the road. A passenger bus stopped next to the altercation. The bus door opened, and several young men jumped off. They promptly broke up the fight, calmly climbed back on the bus, and it continued on its way.

Two days later, I was flying through New York City and read a story in the newspaper about a man who had beat up a woman on a busy sidewalk. Witnesses averted their eyes and walked on. The woman died.

To me, "civilized" means stopping to help versus walkin' on by.

## Ruthlessly Hopeful

Martha Lee was seven when her mom was first diagnosed with cancer and fourteen when her mom's cancer returned and she died. Martha was left insecure, anxious, and heartbroken. Eventually, she recovered enough to function, get married, have three kids, and enjoy a successful career in the nonprofit sector.

Thirty-eight years after her mom's death, Martha's ground shifted. She received a call that she needed a follow-up mammogram because several spots had been detected that required a closer look. The first available appointment was June 10 (her birthday) at 8 a.m. Wham! Buried fears broke through. *I'm going to die, just like my mom.* Her kids would lose their mother, just like she did. What's more, she was really pissed that her fifty-second birthday would begin by being poked, prodded, and squeezed.

After the tests, Martha sat in her paper gown in the exam room, consumed by fear and anxiety. A radiologist came in and said they were going to do a biopsy to see if the spots were malignant. Martha's bottled angst burst out. As she cried, she could barely utter the news that today was her birthday, she was the same age as her mother when she died, and her kids needed their mom. After listening patiently, the radiologist assured Martha that breast cancer treatment was effective, and she explained step-by-step what would happen if the biopsy results were cancerous. Then she shared that ten years ago, she had been diagnosed and treated for stage 4 colon cancer.

What? The radiologist was a glowing picture of health.

Martha's spiral of doom was interrupted. After her biopsy, the technician brought her a piece of coffee cake and wished her a happy birthday. Empathy and compassion in action.

Since Martha knew what to expect, she didn't panic when she received the call confirming her cancer. During treatment, she delved into the science of hope. Her mother's illness and death had taught her that the future isn't always better. Sometimes, it is a whole lot worse. Martha learned that there are steps to help make things better—if not tomorrow, then maybe the next day or the day after that. She founded an organization called Ruthlessly Hopeful to share the process and resources she discovered that cultivate, nurture, and grow hope.

## INDIGENOUS PEACE

During my time with the Hamar, I often sat quietly and observed. I was able to be present in my body, silent, at peace. I believe this was partially because Indigenous people seem to experience the world in a way much older and more complete than what Western science teaches. Indigenous expert Robin Wall Kimmerer explains that while Western science demands objectivity, Indigenous traditional knowledge makes room for and acknowledges human relationships with land. It also respects the innate intelligence of the natural world. "To me," she says, "the power and the promise of traditional knowledge is that traditional knowledge, instead of excluding emotion and spirit, invites it in."[30]

I felt loved and accepted in Hamar. When I relaxed, I started to understand the plight of others from *their* perspective. My mind cleared, and my body became energized. My spirit was light. I could see clearly; the stars were aligned, and my path was illuminated.

---

30   Tim Peterson, "Robin Wall Kimmerer Explains Indigenous Traditional Knowledge," Grand Canyon Trust, April 18, 2023, https://www.grandcanyontrust.org/blog/robin-wall-kimmerer-explains-indigenous-traditional-knowledge.

# DREAM:
## *Activating Empathy and Compassion*

**D**esire: Cultivate the ability to deeply understand and care about the well-being of others.

**R**eflect on the social and physical aspects of their lives.

**E**xplore ways to gain a more complete understanding of the challenges they face.

**A**cknowledge that I need to convert my empathy and understanding into acts of kindness.

**M**antra:
Open my eyes that I might see,
Open my ears that I might hear,
Open my heart that I might feel
The needs and wants of others.

### WISE WOMAN WORDS

"The beauty of the world lies in the diversity of its people."
—*Unknown*

# 12

# Helping Others Help Themselves

There is an ancient Chinese proverb: If you want happiness for an hour, take a nap. If you want happiness for a day, go fishing. If you want happiness for a year, inherit a fortune. If you want happiness for a lifetime, help somebody.

St. Francis of Assisi and Leo Tolstoy suggested the same thing, and Winston Churchill summed it up nicely when he said, "We make a living by what we get; we make a life by what we give."

## HELPING OTHERS FEELS GOOD

Not long ago, if we wanted to learn how to do simple plumbing repairs, clip the dog's toenails, or just about anything, we either called an expert or bought a book. Now we ask Siri or Google or search YouTube. Finding helpful advice is easy, thanks to the folks who post all those do-it-yourself videos. Why do they bother? What motivates them?

Scientific research provides compelling data that helping others is a powerful pathway to personal growth and lasting happiness. Through fMRI technology, we now know that the act of giving activates the same parts of the brain that are stimulated by food and sex. Experiments show evidence that altruism is hardwired in the brain.

It's pleasurable. Helping others may be the secret to living a life that is not only happier but also healthier, wealthier, more productive, and meaningful. Helping others help themselves is particularly thrilling when we can integrate our interests and skills.

It's rare that anyone stumbles upon success without learning some lessons. Sharing what we learned on the way to where we are now—the mistakes we made, ways we simplified or organized our tasks, what we did that worked—can help others achieve their goals. And we, the helpers, experience pleasure and an increased sense of value.

According to mentalhealthcare.org.uk, those of us who are kind and compassionate experience clear benefits to our well-being and happiness. We may even live longer.

## LEARNING TO FISH

One day, my daughter Shay and I were going through a checkout lane at Target when the woman behind us started poking Shay excitedly.

"Shayla, is that really you? Oh my God, I can't believe it. You have changed my life!"

Surprised, Shay and I turned to face a woman around sixty years old, smiling broadly, trailing an oxygen tank behind her. It took Shay only a few seconds to sift through the thousands of students who have funneled through her developmental English classes to recognize a vaguely familiar face.

Marie had struggled to provide for her siblings and then her children for more than fifty years before she had the chance to get her dream job. Shay had gladly spent extra hours with her, teaching her to read and write so that at fifty-five, Marie was finally able to secure work as a clerk at her neighborhood store.

As the famous Chinese philosopher Lao Tzu said, "Give a man a fish and you feed him for a day. Teach him how to fish and you feed him for a lifetime."

On her own time, Shay had patiently taught Marie how to fish!

## HELPING OTHERS HELPS YOU KEEP PERSPECTIVE

Understanding different perspectives not only helps activate empathy and compassion, but it can also enrich one's daily experience.

Try to imagine that you live in California, Texas, Florida, or New York (combined population: 110 million) when disaster strikes. To survive, you must suddenly leave everything you own: property, possessions, and the security of your home and community.

As a woman, you are vulnerable to rape, violence, and exploitation. After facing multiple forms of discrimination, you finally arrive at a border crossing, refugee camp, or host country, expecting asylum. Instead, your security, freedom, and health continue to be threatened. You feel scared and unsettled, overwhelmed by waves of powerlessness.

This is what happened around the world during the first six months of 2023. More than 110 million people were forced to move out of their homes to survive. They were victims of armed conflict, persecution based on religion or ethnicity, development megaprojects that destroyed their homes or livelihoods, extreme poverty, or environmental disasters, such as flooding, earthquakes, and drought.

My heart aches for these people searching for a new home. Please, let's work together to become part of the solution and not turn these vulnerable, scared people away. But for the luck of circumstance and a fortunate zip code, they could be you or me.

## HELPING PEOPLE LEARN FROM FAILURE

It's tricky, even in the best of circumstances, to help someone discover success by understanding their failures. People don't want to be told what they did wrong or why they failed. Daniel Kehrer, in his insightful book *Doing Business Boldly*, uses the metaphor of a "trust" bank account.[31] People make "trust" deposits and withdrawals with each other. Trust accounts need to be full before suggestions on how to learn from mistakes can be heard. Helping someone reflect on what went wrong, and why, and giving them honest feedback is only worth the effort when someone is ready to listen.

As Winston Churchill said, "Success is stumbling from failure to failure with no loss of enthusiasm."

## THE MORE YOU DO FOR OTHERS, THE MORE YOU DO FOR YOURSELF

Helping others gives us a chance to grow. When we gather new knowledge or acquire new data, it's an intellectual exercise. When we have the courage to share what we have learned, regardless of our level of expertise, we internalize our new knowledge. It becomes a part of who we are and gives us the capacity to learn more.

GTLI's major initiatives in Ethiopia involved constructing and refurbishing water schemes and teaching healthy hygiene and sanitation behaviors. During the first three years, we were only able to construct four wells and teach 3,200 people how to prevent and stop chronic diarrhea. But once best practices were identified, our rocket took off. During the next three years, we taught an additional 100,000 people healthy behaviors and constructed or refurbished another 123 water wells.

Ergas provided our rocket fuel.

In Hamar, an erga is a person "who makes it easy for others to understand." Interesting that a language of less than 1,000 words, sounds, and gestures, including tongue clicks and chin pointing, dedicates a specific word to describe a person who helps others help

---

31  Daniel Kehrer, *Doing Business Boldly (Crown, 1989)*.

themselves. The other five South Omo tribes with whom we worked had special words for this as well. Helping each other is a priority.

Many of the best emergent leaders were women. Choosing them as our ergas meant messing around with the underpinnings of an ancient culture. But desperate people do desperate things, and fortunately, money has a loud voice in Hamarland, my nickname for the area. The men decided to risk the ire of their ancestors and agreed. Eventually, we had more than 500 paid ergas, and more than 40 percent of them were women. Community leaders taught other communities that practicing open-field defecation was one of the main reasons they had intestinal problems. The only way they could stop *eating each other's feces* was by using hand-dug pit latrines a distance from their huts. Transmission of germs by the pesky flies would then be diminished, and their drinking water would become less polluted.

GTLI's practice of using ergas to teach healthy hygiene and sanitation behavior was magical for our beneficiaries, the six tribes with whom we worked, and for GTLI. It allowed us to scale our programs rapidly, and it brought outside money into the local economy. It was a win-win.

## GULU'S JOURNEY CONTINUES

Gulu, whom you met previously, became one of our pioneering ergas—the leader of the Minogelti Women's Cooperative, the top student in our functional adult literacy schools, and the role model and leader of the longest operating rural trading center in southern Ethiopia. Recently, our wonderful colleague Yehualashet, who supervises our ongoing orphanage program (www.gtli.us), asked Gulu to describe her life today.

Seven years after GTLI was forced to leave the area, most of the people who went through the healthy hygiene and sanitation training are still practicing healthy behaviors, particularly the women. Gulu reported that they are still successfully operating the rural trading center and grinding mill by themselves, using the basic arithmetic and reading skills they learned in our schools. The trading center earns them enough money to pay for medical care, transportation, and household supplies. The women particularly appreciate the grinding mills because they no longer spend several hours per day grinding grain by hand on a stone slab. The grinding mills generate money, which is shared by the cooperative members.

Gulu expressed that she is glad she took social and economic risks and that the physical violence and death threats were worth it. She is thankful for her community's protection, the support of her children, and the local government workers. She is happy that the law enables her to move around the region freely, teach her children, and work. She feels empowered to make her own decisions and has the right to be involved and participate in community activities.

*Gulu Bola, a woman who has overcome tremendous obstacles to take charge of her destiny, going to market in 2023. My Wonder Woman!*

Gulu made a point of telling Yehualashet that she was terrified during COVID. Not for herself but for me here in the United States. She shared that she walked around holding my picture to her chest, crying and praying that I would be safe. Gulu was more worried about me than herself. Humbling, to say the least.

## HELPING CAN BACKFIRE!

By 2005, rising food prices spurred investors to secure land across Africa. In Ethiopia, where the government offered tax breaks, low rents, and vast tracts of allegedly empty farmland, more land was leased than anywhere else. In August 2020, *The Economist* reported that one study calculated approximately one million hectares allocated between 2005 and 2012, while others suggested it was two or even three times that. The idea was that poor, remote places like South Omo would become paragons of development.

During the time GTLI was working in the area, South Omo became a regular destination for diplomats (major donors, ambassadors, World Bank decision-makers, etc.). They wanted to assess the impact of these "land grabs" since people were being evicted from their land and were losing their livelihoods. USAID does not support resettlement programs, and we were concerned that our "building resilience" initiatives could be misinterpreted as resettlement activity support.

Several of us decided that the best way to persuade key US legislative decision-makers to continue our funding was to facilitate the participation of Gulu and Dobe (Wonga Bayno's key emergent leader) in the United Nations Permanent Forum on Indigenous Issues in May 2015, and then arrange follow-up meetings with select senators and representatives.

With support from the US Embassy in Ethiopia, we managed to get visas for Gulu, Dobe, and Yehualashet (as our interpreter). What a fish-out-of-water experience for Gulu and Dobe. They had to learn how to use Western toilets, eat different food, sleep on beds instead of the ground, and step through a door into a capsule (airplane) that hurtled through the sky. Imagine the faith they had in my ability to keep them safe. It still boggles my mind.

The questions. The wonder of it all. Gulu and Dobe experienced the "magic of yes" as they stepped beyond fear into a startling and different universe. The first morning at breakfast, Gulu leaned over and whispered to me, "Is that a different sun in the sky? Or did it follow us from Hamar?"

The time we spent together in the US exceeded everyone's expectations. My friends met and shared experiences with Indigenous people from around the world and learned about many cultures. Gulu, Dobe, Yehualashet, and I explored New York City together, spent a week in Washington, DC, meeting with legislators and donors, and then flew to Minnesota to meet my family and more supporters. The things that impressed Gulu and Dobe the most were the fat cattle and green grazing lands of the Midwest.

*Dobe (left), Gulu (right) with my granddaughter, Ella, dressed as a Hamar woman.*

Unfortunately, it was a different story when they returned home. Even though we had obtained permission from the elders for Gulu and Dobe's journey, they were furious that GTLI did not give them large sums of money for the loss of Gulu and Dobe's time and attention. Gulu was banished for several months until I was able to travel to Hamar and facilitate some "attitude readjustment." Dobe really suffered. She was physically assaulted when she argued that the money earned by the women should be controlled by women. She was beaten, incarcerated, and separated from her children. It was terrible. But when I saw Dobe later that year, she greeted me with a huge hug and grin. The resilience and innate kindness of these women has significantly changed my behavior. Their example has made me a kinder, more understanding person.

## UNEXPECTED SOURCE OF INSPIRATION

Ideas of how to help others can come from unexpected places. One evening, while sitting in my living room in Addis, the sky suddenly darkened, and I heard a thunderous beating of wings. *Plop! Plop!* Huge grasshoppers fell through my chimney, dropped into my house through open windows, and swarmed through the cracks under my front and back doors. They were massive. At least four inches long and really chunky. Yuk! The swarm of these fat locusts turned day into night. It lasted for at least an hour. I was left with a horrible, sticky mess to clean up.

The "plague experience" generated some new initiative ideas. Intrigued with the idea of a possible food source, I started exploring the viability of grasshopper bread, which led to strategies of harvesting termites. We applied for an innovative grant to convert termites into chicken feed. Although scientific studies showed that chickens eating termite-enhanced food were two times fatter and much healthier than those that didn't, we were turned down because of environmental concerns. Termite mounds were stuck in the middle of unusable scrubland; tough to understand the logic of that decision.

## DONKEYS GET A JOB

We applied for grants to improve health care in South Omo for six years but were turned down until we promised to do the impossible: create demand for family planning.

This objective was in direct opposition to the personal goal of every tribal woman. Wives who didn't have multiple children quickly lost status and were replaced by newer, younger, more fertile women. It was not merely a supposed-to. It was a *must-do*.

Our brilliant behavioral change expert, Delphine Pastiaux-Murphy, developed pictorial community activities that facilitated the discovery of a new phenomenon for adults. They discovered that to have *enough* healthy children to follow their livestock, they had to have *fewer* children, and pregnant mothers needed to eat protein and not walk miles every day, carrying heavy loads. Lots of good messaging to help ease the burden of tribal women.

The element of our initiative that fascinated key donor decision-makers was the donkey ambulances. South Omo covers a vast and difficult-to-access area, which means remote communities do not have access to vehicles. Everyone walks. Health posts are few and far between and not equipped to handle difficult labor.

We convinced the donors (and the local government) that we could save lives by providing donkey ambulances (covered wood wagons with mattresses pulled by a donkey). The program exceeded expectations. The demand for family planning increased, women's lives were saved, and sixteen donkeys, one in each community, finally had a job.

## THE TREE OF LIFE

GTLI's most sustainable initiative was the Moringa Project. In 2015, with funding provided by the UK Department for International Development and supported by the UN's Food and Agricultural Organization, we were able to plant 121,000 moringa trees in the Dassanech region.

Moringa leaflets, consumed fresh, dried, or in powder form, contain high amounts of essential amino acids and micronutrients. Seedlings yield enough leaflets to feed a family within six months, and they increase milk production in dairy cows and stimulate weight gain in beef cattle, breeder chickens, and sheep. The roots are tubular and store water, which people can easily access since the roots run a few inches below and parallel to the surface.

Mature moringa trees were harvested regularly and became a cash crop. Fortunately, it had already become a mainstay food source for most Dassanech people during 2016, when the severe drought otherwise devastated Ethiopia's ability to produce adequate crops.

## HELPING OTHERS CREATES A SENSE OF BELONGING AND REDUCES ISOLATION

Whether volunteering at your local school or food bank or working with marginalized people in Africa, you can make new friends, share common goals, and connect with communities. This helps you create, maintain, and strengthen your social connections.

Jenny Santi, a contributor to *TIME* magazine's Guide to Happiness, wrote "The Secret to Happiness Is Helping Others."[32] She suggests that your passion should be the foundation for your giving, which means choosing what is right for *you* to give.

The gift of time is often appreciated, whether it be a few days, a year,

---

32   Jenny Santi, "The Secret to Happiness Is Helping Others," *TIME*, August 4, 2017, https://time.com/collection-post/4070299/secret-to-happiness/.

or a lifetime of service. Helping others can be the bridge from loneliness and isolation to joy and fulfillment. It certainly has been for me.

## Channeling Energy

Linda Loveland Reid believes her glass is totally full, not just half full, and certainly never empty. At an early age, she decided that being deserted by her mother when she was only two was a good thing because when her dad returned from WWII, he married a wonderful stepmother for her. This also gave Linda a sister who became her best friend and another brother and sister whom she adores. Linda feels she was dealt a lucky hand at birth and suspects that her inspiration to help others comes from knowing her talents are gifts. This belief compels her to use them well and often.

Linda can organize anything and everything. She writes, paints, teaches, motivates, and inspires people. In addition to being a loving mother of three and a successful businesswoman, she carved out time to integrate with her community. She directed community theater in Sonoma and Marin Counties for more than thirty years and is currently a lecturer at local universities and chair of the 250-member Osher Lifelong Learning Art Club. Her paintings are featured in art shows and galleries and grace the walls of historic hotels.

Now in her early eighties, she is still leveraging her gifts of being a successful author (two novels, plus stories, essays, and poems published in thirty anthologies and magazines) to facilitate multiple writer groups and encourage budding authors.

Helping others develop their knowledge and skills

gives Linda purpose, but it doesn't consume her. She is self-aware. She feels she was "blessed with the energy gene," the ability to compartmentalize multiple projects and focus on one thing at a time. The minute she starts feeling overwhelmed, she cancels activities so she can clean out her to-do list. Linda is excellent at resting, nurturing her soul, and finding peace amid chaos.

## AN UNEXPECTED ENDING

I founded GTLI to help these wonderful, forgotten people deal with the challenges they did not create. In turn, they taught me collaboration instead of competition, to overcome my childhood programming, to be open and receptive to love and compassion, to sit quietly and listen, and to become one with nature.

But there was no happy ending for any of us.

After eight years of nonstop involvement and commitment to the tribes of South Omo, I was forced to leave. The tension between the Amhara and Oromo tribes had escalated to the point where it was no longer safe to transport goods and people between Addis and the field.

I ran out of steam at the same time the fighting and killing around me escalated. My friends at the US embassy advised me to take the next plane out. On October 8, 2016, I left with two carry-on bags without saying goodbye to Gulu, Dobe, the other Hamar women, and the elders who had become so dear to me. Even though the organization had accomplished so much, my sense of failure was acute.

I still yearn for my "Star Girls."

The Star Girls of South Omo taught me the importance of opening space for new thoughts, ideas, relationships, and experiences. Of willingly stepping beyond fear to embrace my wise woman within. Their hearts touched mine, causing it to open like flower petals unfolding. The love and trust of Gulu and Dobe paved the way for me to embrace my personal love story (part 4).

Hindsight becomes valuable when we can relax into memories and reflect on lessons learned, allowing them to roll over in our minds and seep into our being. When I expand my memories to include the context of what was happening at a particular time, my self-confidence often gets a boost. More space becomes available for self-love, which in turn increases my sense of well-being.

# DREAM:
## *Helping Others Help Themselves*

**D**esire: Help others realize their potential, foster their autonomy, and increase their self-respect.

**R**eflect on the time and context when someone helped me help myself.

**E**xplore how my experience and resources can foster another person's autonomy.

**A**cknowledge that both the other person and I will reap rewards when they become more self-reliant.

**M**antra:
If I were you,
What would I need to feel worthy?
What would I need to feel secure?

### WISE WOMAN WORDS

"If you have knowledge, let others light their candles in it."
–Margaret Fuller

# PART FOUR

## Find Your Peace

Congratulations! You started life with a unique set of cards, and because of the paths you traveled and the decisions you made, whether by choice or necessity, you are here today—a curious, resilient woman who is committed to finding a sense of peace in your own skin.

According to the latest scientific research, we all have innate wisdom in our cells, passed down through the ages. No matter where and to whom we were born, wisdom resides in our DNA. Even if our wisdom kernel is shriveled and buried under scar tissue, it can be excavated and brought into the light. But it takes work to unravel the tapestry of a life. Patterns have to be identified so lessons can be extracted. Reflection is mandatory: learning requires space and quiet to morph into wisdom.

You may find this difficult to believe. It was for me. And it certainly was tough to do. I had to step out of my comfort zone and embrace life with yet another man. Once I found the courage, I experienced the profound impact of meaningful connections and the transformative power of love. When my environment aligned with my essence, I found peace.

These final chapters share how to reach a state of inner calm, contentment, and harmony. The magic of yes works. With practice and intention, you will find a deeper sense of well-being and balance in your life.

# 13

# Stepping Out of Your Comfort Zone

Our comfort zone is our "home" space, our familiar place. We know the rules and how we need to behave to navigate.

According to Maslow's hierarchy of needs, everyone has multiple comfort zones. Our basic zone includes physiological needs, such as food, water, warmth, rest, and feeling secure and safe. Our psychological zone reflects how we navigate our relationships (our sense of belonging and feeling love) and our need for esteem (how we are perceived by others and feel our own sense of accomplishment). We reach the top of Maslow's pyramid, the self-fulfillment zone, when we maximize our potential and are at peace.

Staying in our comfort zone is like sipping our favorite drink in front of a fire on a cold winter night. The pull to stay where we are is strong, yet never moving means we stagnate and stunt our growth.

As Dr. Margie Warrell explains in *Forbes*, "Growth and comfort can't ride the same horse."[33] She reminds us that we often forget about the risk of *not* taking risks. In other words, we risk missing out on the life we have the potential to live. Opportunities abound, but grabbing hold of them can be scary and difficult.

---

33   Dr. Margie Warrell, "Growth And Comfort Can't Ride the Same Horse," *forbes.com, July 6, 2019, https://www.forbes.com/sites/margiewarrell/2019/07/06/growth-or-comfort-if-you-stick-to-whats-comfortable-you-miss-out-on-whats-possible/.*

## A BIRD TAKES FLIGHT

In "Leaving the Comfort Zone," PositivePsychology.com breaks down the journey into four distinct segments: comfort, fear, learning, and growth.[34]

To progress and grow, we need to pass through the dreaded "fear" zone where our self-confidence becomes susceptible to other peoples' opinions. It is easy to find excuses to not take a risk. According to *Psychology Today*, uncertainty equals danger, which causes fear.[35] Though we may want to expand our comfort zone, the shackle of fear can hold us back.

In 1908, an experiment performed by psychologists Robert Yerkes and John Dodson found an interesting relationship between performance and anxiety. They discovered that mice were more motivated to complete a maze when given mild electrical shocks. However, the mice would hide in fear once the shocks became too strong.

According to the Yerkes–Dodson law, an optimal level of pressure or anxiety increases performance, but only up to a point. Too much pressure has the opposite effect and causes panic. It takes skill to cognitively understand what we are attempting to do and discipline (and time) to put it into practice.

## FINDING MY SWEET SPOT

In 2011, my comfort zone was being alone behind the blue gate when I was in Addis and in my tent or walking along the sandy riverbed

---

34   Oliver Page, MD, "How to Leave Your Comfort Zone and Enter Your 'Growth Zone,'" November 4, 2020, https://positivepsychology.com/comfort-zone/.

35   Brian E. Robinson, "Why You Hate Uncertainty, and How to Cope," *Psychology Today*, November 6, 2020, https://www.psychologytoday.com/us/blog/the-right-mindset/202011/why-you-hate-uncertainty-and-how-to-cope.

when I was in the field. My spirit guides were my companions. When a colleague asked me whether I felt anything was missing in my life, I said no. I felt I was living a diverse life with plenty of stimulation. I was at peace.

I felt less lonely being single. I liked the flexibility of doing what I wanted, with whom I wanted, when I wanted. I promised myself that I would never sit and "endure" again. But if I was so happy, why was I compulsively scrutinizing how couples behaved with each other? Did they look happy? Were they laughing? Were they actively communicating with each other? Usually, the answer was yes.

Hmm. Maybe I was the one missing out.

One Sunday in Addis, when there were no empty tables at a restaurant, I asked a lady seated alone if I could share her table. She agreed, and we started chatting. Soon, a lovely gentleman, John, joined us, and I learned that he and Monica had been lovers for three years, worked together occasionally, and were very happy. Monica mentioned that during the year prior to meeting John, she had asked God to help her be open and grateful if she met a good, suitable partner. She met John—and here they were.

The mere thought of asking my higher power to open my heart to the possibility of becoming involved with another guy gave me the heebie-jeebies! I reacted like an overstimulated mouse in the Yerkes–Dodson experiment; my stomach clenched, my heart raced, and I froze up.

My risk tolerance for another committed relationship was underwater. I was stuck at the second level of Maslow's hierarchy of needs, the psychological zone. Did I even want to muster the courage to conquer this fear? Here I was, finally "unfettered and free." What if the muscle memory of my failed relationships was too much to overcome? Was it worth expending the energy and wasting the time?

On the other hand, it would be nice to feel accepted and loved.

My psychological comfort zone was incredibly small—think matchbox size. It needed to expand exponentially. It took me five years to gradually raise my stress tolerance. I had to use an emotional crowbar to pry open space between the terror of losing my freedom and my emotional reaction to that fear. Lured by the challenge of achieving a new goal, I finally made a commitment. I would try online dating; after all, I controlled the delete key.

## EXPANDING THE ZONE

Stanford psychologist Carol Dweck's book *Mindset* provides a fascinating discussion on two contrasting belief systems: the fixed mindset versus the growth mindset. Over a span of thirty years, her research has shown that the view you adopt for yourself profoundly affects the way you lead your life: "Believing that your qualities are carved in stone—*the fixed mindset*—creates an urgency to prove yourself over and over again. . . . The *growth mindset*, on the other hand, is based on the belief that your basic qualities are things you can cultivate through your efforts, your strategies, and help from others. Although people may differ in every which way—in their initial talents and aptitudes, interests, or temperaments—everyone can change and grow through application and experience."[36]

According to motivational speaker and self-development author Brian Tracy (*Eat That Frog*), "You can only grow if you are willing to feel awkward and uncomfortable when you try something new."

Growth increases resilience. We must equip ourselves to handle change and ambiguity. Sooner or later, shit happens! Life isn't predictable. BetterUp research found that resilience is an inner strength that can be learned. The more we expand beyond our comfort zones, the more we strengthen our resilience muscles. Repeatedly embracing uncomfortable situations builds mental strength, helping us overcome obstacles with more ease and optimism.

Our careers are filled with working through challenges and striving

---

36  Carol S. Dweck, PhD, *Mindset: The New Psychology of Success* (Random House, 2006).

to solve problems. Over time, we acquire new skills and improve our effectiveness. It's strange, then, that so many of us high-achieving women struggle with flexing the same muscles in our personal lives.

Perhaps it's a matter of focus and intention.

"The level of effort you tolerate from yourself will define your life," says Tom Bilyeu, an award-winning screenwriter and entrepreneur. He is so right.

## THE LEARNING CURVE

By the spring of 2016, I knew my time in Ethiopia was ending. Donor funding strategies were changing, harassment by the Ethiopian licensing agency was increasing, and I was running out of steam. I didn't know what the next chapter of my life would look like, but I was ready to find out.

My target date to "flip the page" was January 1, 2017. I wanted to start the new year living someplace else, which I assumed would be somewhere in Africa, and I would fulfill my big supposed-to by writing this book.

My fantasy went something like this: I meet an interesting man on a dating site who is willing to hook up once a quarter in an exciting city somewhere in the world. We spend an exhilarating long weekend together. Then, I fly back to wherever I am living in Africa, and he goes back to where he belongs. I continue being unfettered and free, and no one interferes with my life.

Perfect, eh?

I didn't get many matches, and the ones I did get were duds. My profile messaging read like a grant proposal planning matrix: *this* set of inputs will produce *that* set of outputs, which will yield *these* outcomes. My profile pictures were of Hamar women kissing me on the cheeks and me holding naked babies in the middle of nowhere. Not terribly romantic, to say the least.

I must have subconsciously realized that Abraham Maslow was right when he said, "One can choose to back toward safety or forward toward growth. Growth must be chosen again and again: fear must be overcome again and again."

Once I embraced the possibility of finding someone, my drive to achieve my goal kicked in. I softened my approach and removed the "once a quarter" criterion.

By the time I flew home for a few weeks that summer, my online dating experiment was headed for the trash can. My pursuit of the perfect match was chipping away at the unfettered version of me. I was already making compromises to gain more interest. My profile picture no longer reflected a woman dressed in field clothes, sun-hardened, wearing a baseball cap, and I had switched my location from Ethiopia to Minnesota. Time to slink back to my comfort zone of being alone.

My daughter Shay suggested that before I delete the dating app, my granddaughter Ella and I should check it one last time to see if we could find Ella a new grandpa. Having nothing better to do, we did, and lo and behold, Bill Butcher's profile popped up. Bill wrote that he was looking for a "rare gem" and shared pictures of him running on the beach in Mexico and snorkeling. Ella prompted me to click the button and send a smile.

Bill's experience with online dating was the exact opposite of mine. Unlike me, he wanted to find a partner for the rest of his life. He had just turned seventy-five and was living in Akumal, Mexico, about sixty miles south of Cancun. He hired a professional photographer to snap pictures of him jogging on the beach, bare chested and in shorts, swimming vigorously in the sea, and riding a bike through the jungle. Bill's messaging was articulate and well crafted. He received an avalanche of responses from women ages sixty to ninety across the globe: widows, divorcees, and soon-to-be divorcees. He was offered a life of leisure, living in mansions, flying in private jets, and sailing on yachts.

Bill, a scuba diver for more than fifty years, had made 3,500-plus dives and was a keen fisherman, snorkeler, and body surfer. He wanted to live close to the water, so he methodically eliminated matches from landlocked states in the Midwest. He tells stories of doing triage. When he saw I was from Minnesota, his finger automatically gravitated toward the delete button, but some force (my guides at work) caused him to pause and say to himself, *Oh, I'll just take a quick peek at this one.*

Pictures of me smiling broadly alongside Indigenous women dressed in animal skins and with twisted strands of hair dripping with mud popped up. Another picture showed a dentist sticking a pair of pliers in my mouth in the huge marketplace in Marrakech, Morocco. Bill claims he knew immediately that he had found the love of his life and started developing his campaign strategy. (Bill had a very successful career as a campaign manager.) He immediately shelved his cadre of rich women looking for a "toy boy" and devoted himself to the "Lori Project."

My profile messaging said I was liberal and looking for somebody who knew things I didn't know, was well traveled, curious, and open to experiencing new things. Bill was relieved to discover that I only owned a house near my kids and grandkids in Minnesota but lived in Ethiopia. He was intrigued that I was the founder and CEO of an NGO and thrilled that I was a scuba diver and had traveled the world. He teases me that if I had kept my original profile picture and location as Ethiopia, he would have instantly contacted me.

## THE CAMPAIGN

We both ignored the obvious elephant in the room—me living in Ethiopia and him in Mexico. Instead, our emails and phone calls focused on values and what really mattered to each of us. He wanted a partner and kept assuring me that he knew how to be a good one. I had no clue how to be any kind of partner. For years, I had been a professional boss and a resentful wife. I warned Bill that I wore protective armor and was determined to remain independent.

Bill thoroughly explored our GTLI website and asked good

questions about my work. He even discovered a glitch in our software when he tried to donate from Mexico. Impressed, I felt the first chink in my body armor.

Since I still had a few weeks of leave left, we spent a lot of time on the phone. That was unusual since we both hated long phone calls. We just clicked, with lots to talk about, lots to laugh about, and many enjoyable, heartfelt conversations. He convinced me that he wanted a smart, fun, adventuresome, opinionated partner who wanted conversations that explored ideas rather than just transactional discussions. Unsolicited, Bill promised he would do everything in his power to make me happy. This included not pushing for marriage. I made it very clear that I did not want to be controlled.

I was spending the last weekend of my leave with my son and his wife in Seattle, Washington, and Bill was about to leave on a six-week Mediterranean cargo ship cruise. We agreed to meet under Charles Lindbergh's plane at SeaTac airport.

It became a "fantasy come true" couple of days. I had found the man I never dreamed existed, one with open arms, an open mind, and an open spirit. Bill was fun, loved life, and was ready to embrace the unknown.

When I warned him, "Don't expect me to marry you," he replied, "Why don't we just be unfettered and free together and not worry about the details?"

That plan sounded safe since I was headed back to my house behind the blue gate in Addis Ababa and he was flying to the UK to board a cargo ship. We agreed that at some point during the next six weeks, I would try to join him on the *MSC Flaminia* for a week. The ship's schedule was always in a state of flux, never sure which ports of call would have berths available for ships longer than a football field and carrying over 6,500 containers on a given day. This huge ship had twenty-three crew members and one guest traveler, Bill.

The Filipino crew became Bill's campaign staff. As soon as they were tied up in a port, idle workers would scout for the appropriate SIM card so Bill could call me. One day, the captain notified him that the best place for me to board would be La Spezia, Italy, around October 11. A friend in Addis was flying to Madrid, Spain, on October 8, so I bought a ticket for the same flight.

A few days before my departure, several hundred people were killed during an uprising near Addis. When Bill heard about it, he urged me to consider staying out of Ethiopia for longer than a week. At the last moment, I closed my local bank account, gave all my money to GTLI's finance manager, stuffed my favorite wall hanging into my suitcase, and passed through the blue gate for the last time.

Sometimes, you just gotta have faith!

My two roll-on bags and I said goodbye to my friend when I received word that I had to be in La Spezia at eight o'clock sharp on the morning of the eleventh. I flew to Florence and boarded the train. Unfortunately, I mistakenly took the "milk route" train and arrived in La Spezia late at night with no hotel reservation and unable to speak Italian. Somehow, an honest taxi driver figured out that I needed a room near the cargo port.

Early the next morning, as I struggled to get a taxi, the hotel's night clerk asked me if I'd like him to drive me. When we arrived at the address I had, it turned out to be a closed office. Fortunately, my savior of the day, the desk clerk, recalled seeing an entrance gate at the port and drove there. Praise the guides! It was the right place. My name was on the list, and a driver came to fetch me.

Driving through the container ship port felt like being an ant in a land of giants. Thousands of containers were stacked row after row. Hundreds of truck rigs (tractors) idled there, waiting to be hooked up to a container (often called trailers). When I drove up next to the ship, it towered over me, four stories tall, not counting the stacks of containers.

Bill was right where he said he'd be: hanging over the railing. Literally jumping for joy. The magic of yes! If I had stayed in my comfort zone, if I hadn't pushed through my fear, I would not have been able to experience the amazing state of loving and feeling loved.

According to Dr. Maslow's hierarchy of needs, self-actualization is our need to become everything we can become. It is a continuous journey, not a destination. Many years earlier, Benjamin Franklin shared his thoughts on a similar subject: "Without continual growth and progress, such words as improvement, achievement, and success have no meaning."

## Finding Your Voice

Misty started out living with her parents and brothers in a rusty milk truck that needed to camp in a different place every night since it had no headlights. Embarrassed and ashamed of not being able to shower every day, Misty stayed quiet, fading into the background.

Her parents, noticing her painfully shy manners, encouraged her to take a drama class in high school. In learning a step-by-step strategy to be vocal in front of an audience, magic happened. Misty was able to relax, and her shell crumbled. The light of her personality began to glow between the cracks. She claimed her voice by pretending to be someone else.

Excited to finally be seen and heard, Misty went into overdrive, working every job she could squeeze into her college schedule. Armed with a degree in theater arts, she landed a job in sales and marketing and soon was onstage as her tech company's spokesperson. Gaining experience and honing her public voice, Misty eventually became a member of the leadership team of a Fortune 500 company, as well as their spokesperson. Quite a jump from the girl with no voice to the woman onstage, persuading thousands of people that her company's actions were sound and worthy of investment.

One day, Misty found herself automatically agreeing

to opportunity before intentionally evaluating whether she would stay in alignment with her moral compass by saying yes. She decided to give up her big paycheck and job security and take another leap of faith. She started ToPS (Theatre of Public Speaking), which trains women to effectively communicate one-on-one and one-to-many. They offer individual training, team training, on-demand, as well as membership in the ToPS Speaking Society. Misty knows firsthand the power ready to be unleashed when women find their effective, persuasive voice, acknowledge their worth, and share their knowledge. Have a TED talk coming up? Call Misty.

## CLOSING THE DEAL

When Bill and I disembarked the cargo ship in the UK, I received word from GTLI's board of directors that Ethiopia was too unstable. I was forbidden to return. They urged me to continue my quest to transfer our company's assets and programs to a larger NGO.

Suddenly homeless, I decided to fly back to the States with Bill. I met his family at a gathering in Washington, DC, and then introduced him to my Minnesota clan. Bill's three daughters were delighted that their dad had found someone who made him happy, and my kids were relieved that I was finally leaving Ethiopia.

My attempts to transfer GTLI's programs ran into insurmountable roadblocks. Thanks to the creativity of our US executive director, board members, and wonderful project manager, Yehualashet, we were able to retain our orphanage of mingi children.

Bill and I decided that I would join him in Mexico for a while. There was so much negative energy and vitriol swirling around the 2016 election that we could not stomach the idea of staying in the States. We camped out in his rental unit in Akumal for a few months before buying an adobe house on the beach, south of Mahahual.

Living on a beach in the Caribbean—the dream of all of us old hippies, right? Twenty years ago, Mahahual was a sleepy little fishing village three hours south of Tulum. Then, what soon became the second busiest cruise port in Mexico, Costa Maya, was built a few miles north. Mahahual has become a tourist hub with great restaurants, fun beach activities, and fabulous diving.

Life in paradise was wonderful, but I was weighed down with regret and exhaustion. Intellectually, I knew my time in Ethiopia was over. The government was continuously harassing GTLI, and it looked certain that our annual license would not be renewed. Larger NGOs had moved into our project area and were gobbling up grant money. I hadn't abandoned our beneficiaries by choice, but it sure didn't feel good. It took a long time to forgive myself for leaving people who had come to depend on my advocacy.

Life with Bill kept me afloat. My safe harbor and my lifeline.

## SAYING YES TO THE TURTLE

It didn't take long for me to realize that at our age, Bill and I had to get married. No, I wasn't pregnant. American society, particularly for us senior citizens, is organized for married couples. If one of us had a medical emergency, we wanted to make life decisions for each other. We certainly didn't want arguments about who had access to the person in need. I finally realized that for us, marriage wasn't a supposed-to. It was a legal necessity.

We decided on a beach party rather than another traditional wedding. Bill wrote our wedding vows, a fabricated story about an ancient Mayan marriage custom where turtles were exchanged as a sign of love and commitment. The manager of a nearby beach club was certified to conduct Unitarian marriages, so he became "the man."

Tropical Storm Franklin arrived just as we were ready to party. Our wedding day was spent boarding up the windows of the house and debating whether to convert the beach party to a "boarded-up house" party. At the last minute, we opted for the beach. The eye of the storm cooperated by moving directly over us. The clouds parted, the rain stopped, and we were able to exchange our turtles.

Everyone at the party surrounded Bill and me as we stood under a crooked palm tree. The beach club manager said, "Bill, do you have a turtle to give Lori as a token of your love?" Bill replied, "Oh boy, do I!" and proceeded to fasten an ankle bracelet with a turtle charm around my ankle. We found them online for $8 each.

The DJ cranked up the music, and Bill and I enjoyed our first dance as man and wife to the Etta James classic "At Last!"

But even better than a dream, my new love and life was real.

*Our wedding picture.*

# DREAM:
## *Stepping Out of My Comfort Zone*

**D**esire: Stretch my boundaries and embrace new possibilities.

**R**eflect on the aspects of my life that feel narrow and restricted.

**E**xplore the fears that are preventing me from expanding my reach.

**A**cknowledge that growth is worth stepping beyond fear and embracing the new.

**M**antra:
As my body thaws, the beat of my heart slows,
and I feel fluid.
Aligned, my mind clears, and the wings of possibility
carry my soul.
I rest in the arms of the moon.

### WISE WOMAN WORDS

"Life shrinks or expands in proportion to one's courage."
—*Anais Nin*

# 14

# Embracing Love (and Life)

Bill and I were strolling down a picturesque lane in Akumal when a car abruptly pulled in front of us, both doors opened, and a man and woman jumped out. Fortunately, they didn't have a weapon; they did have a question.

"How long have you been together?"

"Forty years," said Bill.

"Wow."

The man and woman got back in their car and drove away.

I looked at Bill.

"Why did you lie? We've only been together two months."

"Well, that wasn't the answer they wanted."

Giggling, we strolled on, enjoying our day in paradise.

A month later, Bill and I were sitting at the La Luna bar in a small, open square in Akumal. We talked a bit and laughed a lot. Suddenly, a bottle of wine appeared in front of us.

"What? We didn't order this."

The bartender smiled and pointed to two young men sitting across the bar.

"Those guys did."

They smiled and raised their glasses.

Several years later, when we asked for our check in a small café in rural Minnesota, the waiter smiled and shook his head.

"Your check has been paid by that young couple sitting over there."

We hadn't even exchanged glances or smiles with them. What was going on?

It happened again when Bill and I were enjoying each other in a martini bar in downtown San Diego. The onion rings were delicious, and the gin martinis were even better! The couple next to us climbed off their stools and asked a familiar question.

"How long have you guys been married?"

I answer truthfully.

"Seven years."

Bill smiled. I was thirty-three years short, according to his record-keeping.

In each of these instances, we were complete strangers to these kind people. We never exchanged a word or connected in any way. None of these folks knew us or had a clue or insight into our life stories.

What makes seeing Bill and I together so special that ordinary people are motivated to behave in such extraordinary ways? Could the deep love we have for each other be that palpable? Is it possible to witness—and feel—the love shared by two people during a drive-by moment?

If so, as the song says, "What's love got to do with it?"

What role *does* love play? And what is love, anyway?

Love comes in many forms: the love between friends, spouses, partners, relatives, and people and their pets. It can be a transformative and fulfilling experience. Whether it's romantic, familial, or friendship, love releases hormones that make you feel better, plain and simple. Brain chemicals like dopamine and oxytocin can trigger energy and create a sense of attachment when released. This bond can lower blood pressure and stress hormones and improve your overall mood and view of life.

## GETTING READY FOR LOVE

Wayne Dyer, an American self-help guru and motivational speaker, once said, "You don't attract what you want; you attract what you are. You must be what it is that you are seeking; that is, you need to put forth what you want to attract."

Looking back, of course my first marriage was doomed from the start. Not only did Phil and I have little in common to complement each other, but also, I was emotionally stunted. I woke up each day hypervigilant, with my antenna on high alert, guarding against any breach. My mind had iron-grip control. My body was expected to function, and my spirit was ignored. I had no chance of nurturing an emotionally connected, intimate relationship.

The marriage to my second husband, Steve, was doomed as well, embroiled in angst and turmoil. Navigating the chaos of growing JobBOSS while juggling my desire to be a supermom sucked up every ounce of energy. I didn't set appropriate boundaries. Instead of protecting myself from being drained by the demands of others, I exercised like a crazy woman, hoping my body would become as exhausted as my mind. Absolutely the opposite of what medical research recommends. Spending time in nature is what rests the mind, not pedaling furiously on an exercise bike.

It wasn't some magic pill that transformed me from a robot to a person capable of feeling love. It was hard work, fueled by a determination to be the best version of myself. It meant saying yes to navigating through my fear, processing the trauma of my son's horrific accident, overcoming the abuse I suffered as a child, and untangling the knot of angst binding me to Steve. It took over five decades to muster the courage to stand up and advocate for myself.

I made a lot of mistakes and took unnecessary detours, at times moving like a bumbling fool, although occasionally like a woman with grace. But through it all, I was learning. Every bit of the struggle, heartache, and lonely times was worth it. I found solace in planting and nurturing my garden and hiking in the woods. Eventually, rays of light filtered through, calming my mind, and I was able to pause, reflect, and acknowledge, *I am worthy of love.*

---

## EMOTIONAL HEALTH

Well-being is strongly linked to happiness and satisfaction. It comprises a complex combination of a person's physical, mental, emotional, and social health. Without a strong sense of well-being, it is difficult to have a sense of belonging, to trust others and feel confident in your own skin.

According to the World Health Organization, an individual's mental health is considered intact when they recognize their own abilities and can cope with the normal stresses of life. Emotional health, a subset of mental health, refers to a person's ability to manage their thoughts, feelings, and emotions through the ups and downs of daily living. This is key to fostering resiliency and self-awareness.

The state of our emotional health determines how well we interact with others, including how we take in and respond to feedback and criticism and how we observe and interpret what others around us are doing and why. The same skills required to maintain good emotional health are needed to achieve self-love.

Self-love is not about being selfish or conceited. It's about accepting and appreciating ourselves for who we are, flaws and all. It means forgiving ourselves, feeling proud and confident that we have integrity and are behaving with honor and dignity. It means feeling confident in our own worth and abilities, respecting and holding ourselves in esteem.

When we love ourselves, we're less likely to be triggered by the opinions and actions of others. Our boundaries protect us from emotional harm, and in turn, we respect the boundaries of others. As we manage stress, deal with negative emotions, and accept other people's choices, we build strong relationships, which includes providing healthy responses to the physical and emotional needs of others.

## LET'S TALK INTIMACY

Dr. Robert Sternberg, a professor of psychology at Cornell University who is considered one of the most influential psychologists of the twentieth century, developed the triangular theory of love.[37] It posits that the three components of love are intimacy, passion, and commitment.

He defines intimacy as having feelings of closeness, connectedness, and bondedness between two parties. Partners who are intimate can share a whole range of thoughts, feelings, and experiences. They are at ease with each other and feel safe being vulnerable. Intimacy is built over time. It requires patience, effort, and mutual respect. In addition to emotional and sexual intimacy, other forms of intimacy include intellectual, recreational, financial, spiritual, creative, or, in a time of crisis, temporary intimacy.

According to Sternberg's theory, passionate love is based solely on desire. Companionate love, on the other hand, describes a deep connection between two people who care about each other's well-being and are committed to providing ongoing support. Both partners recognize and value each other's individuality, opinions, and feelings. They listen without judgment and show consideration for each other's needs and wishes.

## DELIGHT VERSUS NEED

I married Phil at nineteen, Steve at thirty-five, and Bill at sixty-eight. My three husbands all had very different personalities, educational backgrounds, and childhoods. The first two marriages failed, and the third was (and remains) a wild success. Why? Each of us had different

---

[37] The Sternberg Center for Successful Relationships, "The Love Profile—Three Components That Matter in Every Relationship," https://lovemultiverse.com/understanding-love/kinds-of-love-profiles/.

preferences, interests, and abilities. Some were complementary and some were at odds. Those differences mattered, but they were not the root cause of my failed marriages or the reason I finally found my heart's delight.

I married Phil and Steve because of need. Phil and I started out as pen pals. He was stationed in Vietnam when I was an eighteen-year-old living alone in Los Angeles. Neither of us were emotionally healthy or capable of helping each other grow and develop. According to Maslow's hierarchy, we were in the lower two tiers of the pyramid (physiological and safety needs).

I married Steve while I was still stuck there. It wasn't until I was in my fifties that I was able to crawl up to the third tier (love and belonging) and fourth (esteem) of Maslow's pyramid. I didn't jettison the weight of my second marriage until I was sixty years old. Only then was I able to approach tier five (self-actualization).

During my years in Ethiopia, my guides helped my heart heal. I had time and mind space to question, reflect, and finally understand my feelings and actions. My heart opened and enlarged, able to hold the good with the bad. Over time, I grew to acknowledge my innate goodness. My self-image transformed from a possessed, sinful creature to a person with a loving soul and spirit and pure intentions. I started to nurture, value, and love the essence of me.

I found peace.

When Bill popped up as a match on the dating site, my heart was already healthy. I was equipped to welcome him and embrace his essence. I didn't *need* him to satisfy my emotional needs. We both were at peace. Our mutual desire was to experience the joy of sharing . . . and have fun.

## LOVE MATTERS!

We are surrounded by movies, books, and constant chatter about love. Humans are wired for this connection, and when we cultivate good relationships, the rewards are immense.

"There's no evidence that the intense, passionate stage of a new romance is beneficial to health," says Harry T. Reis, PhD, coeditor of the *Encyclopedia of Human Relationships*.[38] Meanwhile, "people who participate in satisfying, long-term relationships fare better on a whole variety of health measures." The key is to "feel connected to other people, feel respected and valued by other people, and feel a sense of belonging."

The most common health benefits linked to loving relationships are better stress management, increased life expectancy, and boosting the immune system. Having the security and support of a partner or close friend to help you through difficult situations and emotions can lower your blood pressure. MRI scans have shown that those in stable relationships have greater activity in the part of the brain responsible for the reward/pleasure response and less activation in the area associated with anxiety. Tensions ease when you feel love and support, and evidence suggests that sleep improves, too, allowing you to feel refreshed when you wake up.

A blog article from the University of Texas health program supports the notion that those involved in healthy social relationships increase their life expectancy.[39] "The Surprising Health Benefits of Love" by Lauryn Gerard claims that these relationships can even lower one's risk of developing cardiovascular disease, certain types of cancer, and pneumonia. In 148 studies with more than 300,000 participants, those with the strongest social relationships had 50 percent increased longevity over those who didn't have strong social networks.

If your social network doesn't feel up to par, no need to panic. Meditating on love can slow down the aging process. Researchers have discovered that people who practice loving-kindness meditation, which focuses on kindness and warmth toward others, have longer

---

38  Sherry Rauh, "10 Surprising Health Benefits of Love," WebMD, January 29, 2009, https://www.webmd.com/sex-relationships/features/health-benefits.
39  Lauryn Gerard, "The Surprising Health Benefits of Love," UT Health Austin, February 13, 2019, https://uthealthaustin.org/blog/health-benefits-of-love.

telomeres, the segments of DNA that control aging. Shorter-than-average telomeres have been associated with accelerated aging and a shorter lifespan, so the longer, the better.

With regards to the immune system, long-term companionate love can reduce the chance of catching a cold and other infections. Eighty percent of our immune system (and the vast majority of our bodies' microbes) resides in the gut, which is partially regulated by immunoglobulin A, an antibody that has been shown to decrease the risk of cancer. Overall, the bond between people and their pets can likewise positively impact both emotional and physical well-being. In fact, researchers have discovered that college students who spent just eighteen minutes petting a dog showed significant increases in this same antibody. The feeling of love helps nurture and support life-enhancing gut microbiome and fights off harmful bacteria.

## CELEBRATE YOUR LIFE

In *Psychology Today*, award-winning author and journalist John-Manuel Andriote encourages us to live our lives strongly by being true to our authentic selves, willing to stand out from others.[40] This means risking others' disapproval or rejection when we act according to our own judgment and values, not those prescribed without our consent, perhaps even before we were born.

When we embrace life, we are at home with ourselves. We accept where we are on our life journeys and don't measure our progress by anyone else's standards. Only we know how far we have come because we know where our journeys began, the obstacles we overcame, and the suffering we endured. There is no need to pretend to be anyone.

---

40   John-Manuel Andriote, "What It Means to Embrace Your Life and the Path You Chose," *Psychology Today*, January 22, 2022, https://www.psychologytoday.com/us/blog/stonewall-strong/202201/what-it-means-to-embrace-your-life-and-the-path-you-chose.

We enjoy being who and what we are, as authentic with others as we are with ourselves. We find peace within ourselves.

If you've reached this point, you're ready to bring yourself fully into each day, open to absorb all it has to offer. Instead of relentlessly pursuing things (better job, bigger house, new stuff to fill it with, etc.), choose to express thankfulness for what you *do* have. Leaning into the good in life shifts your attention away from the negative. Consciously and actively enjoying where you are and what you have relaxes you and helps you find the beauty in the ordinary.

Fun is often the key to enjoying life. Embrace the unconventional. Create the unexpected. Try to cultivate a mindset that embraces play, pleasure, and laughter every single day. Here are some tips to insert more fun into your life.

1. *Seek out laughter.*

Watch funny movies, TV shows, or stand-up comedy that makes you laugh. Laughing usually means you're having fun. Share funny content with others to spread laughter. One of Bill's older friends (Jules is in his late eighties) routinely sends out a collection of funny pictures and jokes. Both of us chuckle as we scroll through them.

2. *Learn to laugh at yourself.*

Bill is a master of this. He thinks he is hilarious. Instead of getting frustrated when he forgets something or struggles with a simple task, he laughs, picks himself up, and moves on. He is a cheerful, optimistic, and resilient man.

*Mr. Spontaneous finds "fun" in most situations!*

3. *Enjoy little moments in your everyday life.*

Allow yourself to have small moments of fun during your day in five-to-ten-minute increments. Make time for tiny breaks to indulge in small pleasures. In our house, this generally means throwing the ring for Moonie, our lovely, energetic cattle dog. Her tail wags nonstop whenever she sees me carrying a clothes basket into the bedroom, the designated ring-throwing room. (It has carpet.) She jumps, twirls, and scrambles after that red ring, determined to get in as many throws as possible during the time it takes me to fold a load of clothes. Her joy and enthusiasm thrill me. It's fun for both of us.

4. *Be spontaneous in the moment.*

Not all fun activities have to be planned or scheduled. Being open to new, unplanned experiences brings unexpected fun and delight. One night, when Bill and I were walking down a sidewalk in Mexico, we heard music from a bar across the street. Suddenly, Bill grabbed my hand and twirled me around, leading me through our favorite dance moves. And now that Bill has balance issues and uses a walker, that night remains a special memory. We still dance in a public swimming pool while Bill hums the tune.

5. *Seek out and try new things.*

Grab any chance to try something new, no matter how small. A young, introverted scientist friend, Jake, shared that he forces himself to participate in an improv class. He recognized that he wasn't having much fun in his daily life, that he was not connecting with people. Jake wanted to "lighten up," so he stepped out of his comfort zone. Brave man.

6. *Adjust your mindset to think more positively.*

Optimistic people have more fun than pessimistic thinkers. Try to imagine a positive result instead of what you fear will happen. I love the scene Daniel Kehrer describes in his book *Doing Business Boldly*: "A man in hell can hear a loud, raucous party in heaven, which is on the other side of the mountain. He groans forlornly, bitter with regret, and screams as he suffers the fire and brimstone of hell. The man doesn't realize that the mountain is on wheels and all he must do to join the fun in heaven is to push the mountain aside."[41]

Try asking yourself when confronted with an insurmountable roadblock: *Could this mountain possibly be on wheels?*

Surprisingly often, the answer is yes.

Set the obstacle aside while you work through the other issues, and *voilà!* A new path appears, and you figure out a workable detour around the roadblock.

---

41   Kehrer, *Doing Business Boldly.*

Being optimistic inspires those around you. Finding ways to have fun is powerful. It has certainly worked its magic on me. Bill's consistent optimism is infectious. Instead of regretting that he can no longer hike, help with household chores, or open my car door, he thinks about how lucky he has been, remembering all his good experiences. His commitment to being positive and having fun shines a brighter light into my life.

### Different Kinds of Love

Teralyn reminds me of Sandy, Olivia Newton John's character in the musical *Grease*. Sparkling blue eyes, blond ponytail, full of energy. She was a happy kid with lots of friends, a good student, and had no major issues at home. Her passion was drama, and she often starred in high school plays and community theater. Teralyn's screenwriter friend living in LA asked if she wanted to rent his empty bedroom and try auditioning for parts in movies. Since she had just graduated and didn't have full-time work, she decided to give it a try.

It was fun for a while, and she landed several bit parts, but she soon tired of the "sleep with me and I'll get you an audition" pressure. Teralyn had boyfriends but no one serious. She found it tough to make enough money to support herself and tougher to feel valued for herself. After a few years, disgusted with the whole movie-making scene, she moved back home and was soon working as a checkout clerk at the local Trader Joe's.

Sparks flew when Teralyn and Haley, another checkout clerk, first spotted each other. They instantly knew they wanted to be partners for life and were soon married. When Teralyn talks about Haley, her sparkle shines brighter and she glows.

The other day, when I was chatting with some ladies in my art class, I mentioned that Bill and I had met online. The ladies eagerly chimed in with their stories. Oona smiled and said she was happy she was living with her ex-husband again. Kar beamed and told us that she and her husband have been happily married for fifty-four years. Barbara added that she and her ex-husband have lived 2,000 miles apart for years but still celebrate special occasions together with their kids. Gail, our teacher, grinned and talked about how thrilled she is to be single, living near her granddaughter and making art. When I spoke with my daughter Melissa that night, she told me she now sleeps horizontally across her bed so her three cats can be comfortable.

Love for another being is not one-size-fits-all. When we open our hearts, embrace the moment, and let possibilities happen, it is custom-made.

## CHOOSE JOY

My guides routinely lead me to thought-provoking articles. One spring, they directed my attention to a commencement address given by Rebecca Fielding-Miller, an associate professor at UC San Diego Herbert Wertheim School of Public Health, that was published in the *San Diego Union Tribune*:[42]

> Choose the people who give you joy, and the hobbies that give you joy, and the sights and the sounds and the smells and the tastes and the feelings and the places that give you joy. Choose

---

[42] Rebecca Fielding-Miller, "10+ thinkers, 200 words, one question: What's your advice for San Diego College Grads?" *San Diego Union Tribune*, May 25, 2023.

to bring more joy into the world by being kind and making something beautiful. You are at the beginning of something new. There is no map. There are no rules. There is only you and the relationships you have built, and the things you have learned so far. How wonderful. Good luck. We're all cheering for you.

I'm cheering for you to find your own joy. May your cup runneth over!

# DREAM:
*Embracing Love (and Life)*

**D**esire: Embrace my life with eager anticipation and delight.

**R**eflect on moments and events that cause me to laugh and (want to) dance for joy.

**E**xplore and seek out opportunities when I can laugh at myself in front of others.

**A**cknowledge that when I smile and greet others first, I may shine a light on their day.

**M**antra:
Let me love and live
With a sunny blend of tolerance,
Arms wide open,
Eager to embrace the day.

## WISE WOMAN WORDS

*"You're not happy unless you think you are."*
—Gretchen Kucher

# 15

# Weeding Your Physiological Garden

Creating a tranquil garden requires work—the right selection of plants for the weather and soil as well as careful pruning, weeding, and watering. One's interior garden (body, mind, and spirit) needs similar attention to reach its fullest potential and thrive. For me, that meant getting rid of unwanted weeds (thoughts and beliefs) that had taken root in my mind, and now that I was no longer numb, my body was a discordant symphony of aches and pains. My soul yearned for nurturing and loving care.

Bill and I thought we had purchased our forever home when we decided to exchange living on the beach in a remote area of Mexico to a high-rise condo in downtown San Diego. We finally acknowledged that at our age, access to quality health care was a must. San Diego seemed ideal because of its diversity, proximity to Mexico, seventy-five miles of coastline, entertainment, and weather.

We were happy, content, and snuggled in until we took our June 2023 trip to explore the national parks of California.

As we shared our customary bottle of wine during our first evening in a B-and-B nestled in the woods with soaring windows and scant floor space, Bill suddenly asked a provocative question, one of his fascinating traits.

"Why aren't we living in a place like this? We both love the peace and serenity of nature."

My instant reaction was joy. Bill had always maintained that living close to, on top of, or under the sea was a must for him. There had never been a whisper that he might consider living in the woods away from the sea. But once he uttered those words, a new path appeared. Compelled to explore, we immediately started our search for a house in the woods anywhere in the USA with access to good food and a decent airport.

Clinging to the idea that we were already living in our forever home never occurred to us. We loved sitting in our ratty recliners and looking out over "America's Finest City," but the vibrancy of an urban setting couldn't compete with nature. What difference did it make that we were in our seventies and eighties?

But wait. The elevator outside our door in San Diego provided easy access to the lobby and underground parking. Bill was independent, able to maneuver easily with his walker or mobility scooter. We could access restaurants, theaters, or the ballpark. Why leave our ultraconvenient life for the unknown?

The simple answer was, why not? The desire to align our essences with our environment was more important to our well-being than avoiding the complexities of moving and worrying about accessibility. We decided to act on our impulse for adventure and change and not let the fact that I was scheduled for a knee replacement slow us down. After all, speed bumps happen.

We chose the magic of yes.

## PESKY WEEDS

I love to garden but not to weed. Thinking about flowers, shrubs, and trees, meandering through garden centers, and imagining how the combinations of foliage textures and colors will look makes me happy.

Pruning, shaping trees and shrubs, cutting flowers and arranging them, all good. But not weeding. I want it done but don't like doing it.

Our gardens often provide a window into our lives. My gardens have varied widely, changing with the ebb and flow of my experiences. The one variable that never changes, however, is that for a garden to thrive, it has to be congruent with the environment. What's planted in Minnesota won't work on the beach in Mexico. We all know that climate and soil make a huge difference. Same holds true for us. To grow and blossom, we need to pay attention to where we are planted. And even though it makes us uncomfortable and itchy, everything that gets in the way of being the person we strive to be needs to be weeded out of our lives. Anything that sucks our energy, depletes our souls, fills our minds with negative thoughts, or impedes our growth needs to be closely examined and dealt with immediately and definitively.

Weeds choke life.

The mind and spirit need healthy nutrients just like our bodies need fruit, vegetables, and exercise. Violence, angst, and mayhem assault the immune systems. Our surroundings (people, entertainment, activities, things that creep into our minds) leech into us, affecting every fiber of our being.

Our environment declares our essence. Peaceful surroundings foster a tranquil mind, kindness encourages love, and consideration promotes harmony.

Sounds lovely and serene, but how do we make it happen when the mind is in charge of all decisions and treats the body and spirit as nonentities? During the first fifty-five years of my life, my environment (friends, acquaintances and colleagues, movies I watched, books I read, men I married) was fragmented and scattered. No wonder my mind was always busy. Rest and sleep were elusive, and the only emotions I felt were loneliness and anxiety. The journey to corral and align these random factors has been arduous. Rocky at times but well worth the struggle. It's paid amazing dividends, and I finally feel at peace. The steps are deceptively simple.

## STEP #1: ACCEPTANCE

First, I had to acknowledge that I was out of whack. Since my mind controlled everything, my body and spirit didn't get a vote. My being was so out of alignment that when I had the flu and was nauseous, my mind wouldn't let my body vomit. I had to faint first. This happened three different times. What's more, I was seven months pregnant with my son before I acknowledged that the frequent movement in my abdomen was my baby kicking. True story, and I'd already had two children. I wasn't *supposed to* get pregnant if I wasn't married; therefore, I wasn't pregnant. Mind over matter, no problem whenever it served my purposes.

## STEP #2: SURRENDER

Next step, thaw out my numb body. I worked with a great somatic therapist on Bainbridge Island, Washington. Sharon Stanley gently and methodically helped me release the unresolved trauma stored in my body. Facilitated by her expert guidance, my legs quivered, my arms shook, and my body awakened. Fascinating process. Life-changing. Much more effective for me than "talk" therapy. Over time, I felt the pleasure of a sudden breeze and happiness when something delighted me, and my hypervigilance abated. It became easier to breathe.

Late one night, while I was trying to fall asleep in Ethiopia, I had an epiphany. I saw my being as three different entities: mind, body, and spirit. I realized that my mind was a big-time bully, always needing to be in charge, making all the decisions, totally discounting the needs of my body and spirit.

It was time for a heartfelt apology. Lying in bed, we had a ceremony. My mind apologized to my spirit and my body and solemnly promised to step back and let the other parts of my being develop. The three of them defined their roles:

*Mind*: My thinking mind runs the spreadsheets, does the research, asks the questions, processes data. It is a staff position, a supporting actor, not the lead.

*Body*: My physical body is the bellwether, the key indicator or metric.

It tells me how I am feeling about what I am experiencing and doing.

*Spirit*: My spirit is the message center, the compass, the moral guide. It tells me if I am on the right track. It is the keeper of my intuition, the guardian of my soul.

It works pretty well, most of the time . . .

## STEP #3: DISCOVERY

I needed to discover my essence, my true, authentic self, before I could align my essence with my environment. Fran Fisher, a master certified coach, explains this concept well:[43]

> Your essence drives your way of thinking, your values, your actions and ultimately your life path, whether you are conscious of it or not. Your essential nature is not your identity. It is not your body, appearance, your nationality, nor your roles in life. It is not your work. It is not your thoughts, feelings, character, or personality. All those aspects are vulnerable to change and circumstances. Your essence is the unalterable *truth of your being*. Uncovering your essential nature will shift your world view—your life orientation—and give you greater access to your authentic power—the power to positively and consciously shape your life by making day to day choices that leverage your innate strengths and the intrinsic qualities that make you "*you*."

Andrea Spyros, author of the blog article "The Four Pillars of Alignment: A Psychoactive Framework for Personal Growth," says, "When you are in alignment, the infinite energy flows gracefully around and through you. When you're not in alignment, life can feel like a struggle."[44]

---

[43] Fran Fisher, "Uncover Your Essence and Discover WHO You ARE," LinkedIn, July 27, 2018, https://www.linkedin.com/pulse/uncover-your-essence-discover-who-you-fisher-master-certified-coach.

[44] Andrea Spyros, "The Four Pillars of Alignment: A Psychoactive Framework for Personal Growth," Brainz, July 14, 2022, https://www.brainzmagazine.com/post/the-four-pillars-of-alignment-a-psychoactive-framework-for-personal-growth.

When our cars need a front-end alignment, we know it. Tough to steer, not fun to drive. When we have a leg or foot in a cast, it's hard to walk, and our backs ache. Most people know when something physical is out of alignment. Few people know when their essence is out of whack, even though it causes unnecessary struggles. Being in alignment allows us to live our lives to their fullest potential. We'll still face challenges when aligned, but we will have more resources and tools to overcome them.

∽

## THIS BODY HAS *FEELINGS*

We constantly hear and read about the importance of exercise, eating a nutritious diet, and getting enough sleep. I don't recall seeing or hearing much about the importance of feeling sensations in the body. If we are not aware and do not acknowledge what is happening in our bodies, how do we really know what is going on?

I only started to feel sensations other than anxiety and fear in my midfifties, after doing a lot of personal work. There is no magic pill. To achieve a sense of well-being and tranquility, we must undertake an intentional process.

Mine was guided by this mantra gifted to me by my shaman in June 2010:

> Lady of the sweet water of the river
> Renew in my being the endless source of love, peace, and harmony.
> Hail Oxum in the sky, on the Land, in the Water.
> Shield me with your Love.

I repeated my mantra multiple times a day for months before I stopped and really thought about what I was asking for. What did it really mean to be an endless source of love, peace, and harmony? And how could a die-hard, competitive workaholic morph into such an alien being?

I was comforted by the word "restore." It meant that at some point in my existence I had been a source of those qualities I wished to emanate. Somewhere inside me there had to exist at least a tiny cellular memory of how I could be loving, peaceful, and harmonious.

Picturing success in this endeavor became much easier after I met Bill. At least then I knew what love for a partner looked like. It took a while to realize that the best way I could show my love for my kids was to *not* give them advice. Love meant lending support by facilitating their ability to do well—finding ways to release their potential, to help them soar independently.

Google defines peace as "free from disturbance, being in the state of tranquility or quiet." For me, peace means being in an unvigilant state, free from fear and doubt, able to relax into the moment. Feeling safe enough to trust, to give up control. The mind is quiet, free from tension and stress. Feeling at peace in nature is easy. Feeling at peace amid chaos is a challenge.

Harmony is a human value that refers to compatibility and accord in our feelings, actions, relationships, opinions, and interests. It denotes a state of balance among forces influencing and even opposing one another. Harmony requires alignment. All elements are complementary and absent of friction. There is free-flowing energy between them and no rub, no bottlenecks, no disconnects. The whole is better than the sum of the parts, improved by being integrated.

Each of us can influence harmony in our body. It is determined by what we ingest and what we do to keep our bodies functioning at peak performance. For me, that includes not eating most meats. I don't want the energy of animals to interfere with my own. This was an easy decision and transition. I've always preferred fruits, vegetables, seafood, and fowl, but I never touched beef again after a cow was slaughtered one holiday morning in Addis underneath my open window. I heard a terrible bellow, and when I looked out, I saw a group of neighborhood men whooping and hollering as they cut up the cow. They ate the raw meat while it was still warm and dripping blood. That did it. Decision made.

You may wonder why I still eat seafood and fowl. I love the taste and texture, so I've decided to believe that sea creatures and fowl don't have souls. Funny how we can rationalize our decisions even when we know we are not being logical.

## TWO-SIDED MIND

The state of mind reminds me of a pendulum. When the pendulum is hanging straight down, at rest, the mind is quiet, at peace. When it is at the forty-five-degree "busy" angle, it is consumed with critiquing conversations and actions, reliving regrets of the past, and planning for tomorrow or the distant future. Conversely, when the pendulum is at the forty-five-degree "mental fatigue" angle, it is mired in mush, overworked, unable to think clearly or process efficiently.

For years, my mind was stuck in the busy mode. I was always reviewing and critiquing every conversation I had and action I took. I rationalized I was practicing continuous improvement. Wrong. It was self-flagellation. I was vigorously beating myself up. Intellectually I knew that I always meant well and never intentionally caused people harm. But it took years to convince my mind to stop berating itself.

Reciting my mantra redirected my thoughts and calmed the busy chatter. By repeating, "Peace, love, harmony" three times as soon as an unwanted thought popped up, my downward spiral stopped. Whack the negative thoughts with good intentions, and your mind will stop circling the drain.

Mental fatigue is a sign of needing to "drop out," to give yourself permission to not participate. When your ability to process slows down, it's time to take a break and stop solving problems, helping others, and doing what is expected of you. Give yourself the gift of taking care of *you*. Recharge. My magical recharge methods include walking our dog in the woods or swimming laps in the neighborhood pool. My mind relaxes, and new ideas have the space to percolate.

## The Body Journey

Tonia and her sister, Tiffany, planned to move away from home as soon as they turned nine and fourteen. Tiffany had a fake ID. Both started working at an early age, made dinner for themselves every night, and rebelled in school. They were tough and invincible. Their single mom was too busy to notice. She was going to nursing school, working full-time, and listening to lectures on tape while sewing the girls' clothes. Their dad showed up every few weeks to do something fun.

One day, the ground shifted under the girls' feet. Their dad remarried and started to attend personal growth workshops. When he began teaching others how to understand their behavior, he became aware of his independent daughters' scheming and plotting. He abruptly switched from being "Disneyland dad" to "personal growth dad."

Days spent enjoying rides and treats at the amusement park were replaced with hitting pillows and being encouraged to see themselves as the creators of their circumstances instead of victims of events instigated by their parents and teachers.

Tonia discovered her personal power when she let go of resentments and dropped her emotional baggage. Determined to be as powerful as possible, she decided to do Tony Robbins's fire walk. She heard she would get more out of his Unleash the Power Within workshop if she paid for it herself, so fourteen-year-old Tonia worked 150 hours to make sure she got the most out of walking barefoot over hot coals. She wanted to prove she had the courage to take on any challenge. After her fire walk, mind over matter became ingrained. Tonia the Invincible.

This tough, independent woman started giving massages when she was twenty-two. She had no idea that body work would become her career. Today, Tonia Lach's therapeutic Body Journey incorporates sound healing, prayer, touch, deep massage, and energy release. She opens all the Chinese meridians so that energy from the earth can come up and out, allowing the recipient to serve with their hands and heart. The Body Journey aligns a client with their creativity and art in this world, whether their art is cleaning, running spreadsheets, or building rockets to go to the moon.

Tonia has given her life over to shamanic prayer. She wants to help create the world she craves by embodying it, praying for it, and envisioning it. She is happiest when she is in a state of gratitude and prayer.

## SPIRITS CAN SOAR

When I mention "spirit," I'm not talking about a spiritual or religious concept here. Think about your spirit as being your vibe, the energy of your life force. Your spirit does not care what you believe. It only cares about the essence of *you*. It is the part of you that senses when you are in or out of alignment. It is the eyes of your soul, looking inward. When I am assaulted by negative energy that forces me out of alignment, I often become angry, irritated, and experience an upset stomach or a strong sense of overwhelm. My spirit causes my body to reject what is happening to it or around it.

Moral injury is the psychic damage created by taking part in something that violates our souls, something contrary to our values. When we are aligned with our spirits, however, our life force flows like a river, free and unimpeded.

## ENVIRONMENT: INSIDE AND OUT

The words we hear, the sights we see, the aromas we smell, the elements we feel, and what we ingest all impact us profoundly. Environment is within us and outside us. It enfolds us, body, mind, and spirit.

Fran Fischer, a master certified coach, discusses the concept of living from the "outside in" versus the "inside out" in her article titled "Living from the Inside Out" published in *Choice*, the magazine of professional coaching.[45] She contrasts living according to external expectations and consistently accommodating others to do what they want or expect (outside in) with living from our own internal values and authentic selves (inside out). She encourages us to align our lives with our inner truth and values rather than external validation or societal norms. Living outside in is exhausting and discouraging. Living inside out is energizing and fulfilling.

Switching my orientation from outside in to inside out requires a lot of intentional practice. I am grateful that I am able to plug into the energy of my guides.

---

45  Fran Fischer, "Living from the Inside Out," *Choice, Spring 2013.*

# DREAM:
## *Weeding My Physiological Garden*

**D**esire: Adapt my environment to align with my core values.

**R**eflect on the times I feel surrounded by nurturing, positive energy.

**E**xplore how I feel when I am with my friends, my colleagues, and resting at home.

**A**cknowledge that I may need to make some changes.

**M**antra:
I am happy.
I do not want. I am not seeking.
I feel at home.
I am not lonely. I feel complete,
Loved, at peace, in harmony with my being.

### WISE WOMAN WORDS

"I invite you to breathe life into your dreams,
to water them tenderly from the deep reservoirs you hold
within, and to guard them fiercely."
—*Sarah Livia Brightwood Szekely*

# 16

# Recognizing the Wise Woman Within

I believe these truths are worth repeating: You don't have to be old to be wise. Traveling the world is not mandatory. Miles on your body, entry stamps on your passport, and wrinkles on your face don't guarantee wisdom. They merely tell the story that you have been lucky to have adventures and are eligible for senior citizen discounts.

Each of us has inner wisdom. It resides in our cells, our genes, and our memories. Research indicates that it's not merely the events of our lives that shape our wisdom but how we reflect on them. If we want our experience to translate into wisdom, we must commit to pulling apart the threads of our life tapestries. Only then can we identify patterns and extract valuable lessons.

The ancient philosopher Plato cautioned us in this regard when he said, "Let no one be slow to seek wisdom when she is young, nor weary in the search of it when she has grown old. For no age is too early or too late for the health of the soul."

Jon Gruda, PhD, associate professor of organizational behavior at Universidade Católica Portuguesa, teaches that quality and depth enable us to reflect on our memories and that intensity, sincerity, and purpose are vital to this retrospection. True wisdom emerges by reflecting deeply on these experiences, using our insights to guide our thoughts and actions. This is not a fast or efficient process. It takes time, patience, and a determination to be brutally honest, rooted in the desire for self-improvement.

Cultivating wisdom is easier today, thanks to accessible resources. In 2019, *The Harvard Review of Psychiatry* published "The Emerging Empirical Science of Wisdom: Definition, Measurement, Neurobiology, Longevity, and Interventions."[46] The article affirms that the science of wisdom is the science of all sciences!

While attending a recent lecture on the cellular transmission of wisdom, I was thrilled to hear that conclusions drawn by esteemed researchers are very similar to what we intuitively know. We women are wise. We just need to acknowledge this fact and practice accessing our wise woman within. Legions of wise women who have walked this earth and thousands who are alive today, perhaps next door, are ready to show us the way. We merely need to say three simple words: "Please mentor me."

## WISDOM SEEKER

This is the recipe to activate your wise woman within: Seek knowledge. Be open-minded. Self-reflect.

1. *Seek knowledge.*

Open the space for new thoughts, ideas, experiences, and relationships. Research shows that wise individuals have a thirst for exploring different perspectives and delving into foreign cultures. As mentioned previously, reading books is an excellent alternative to travel. I marvel at how accurately Barbara Kingsolver describes the challenges of living in a remote African village in *The Poisonwood Bible*, and Tan Twan Eng teaches us about Malaysia in his captivating books *The Gift of Rain* and *The House of Doors*.

---

46   Dilip V. Jeste and Ellen E. Lee, "The Emerging Empirical Science of Wisdom: Definition, Measurement, Neurobiology, Longevity, and Interventions," *The Harvard Review of Psychiatry*, 2019 May/Jun; 27(3):127–140.

Twenty years ago, Jared Diamond's *Guns, Germs, and Steel* ignited my thirst for anthropology. Podcasts, online courses, and adult classes at a neighborhood school can provide wonderful opportunities to explore new topics of interest. Seeking knowledge also includes being open to feedback from others. Surround yourself with people who challenge you, support your growth, and offer constructive criticism.

2. *Be open-minded.*

Being receptive to ideas and perspectives, along with exercising relentless curiosity, will allow you to analyze problems from a new angle. These traits of open-mindedness are not comfortable for everyone. Sally, a relative of mine, often accuses people of yelling at her whenever they calmly disagree with her opinions. She doesn't want anyone to ask questions or offer a different point of view. Because she focuses only on what she knows, she limits her ability to expand her mindset. Hopefully, Sally will eventually stop feeling threatened and open her mind to the words of Imre Lakatos, a Hungarian philosopher of mathematics and science, who said that "no degree of commitment to beliefs makes them knowledge."[47]

3. *Self-reflect.*

Reflection helps you clarify your values, beliefs, and uncover biases and personal limitations. While living in Ethiopia, I was humbled (and surprised) when my hidden prejudices kept popping up. Brutal self-examination of those biases provided insights into myself and helped me understand others better. Every day, something reminds me that my personal knowledge is limited and there is so much more to learn. When I remember to question my views and behavior nondefensively, I find that my point of view broadens and becomes less self-serving.

---

[47] Imre Lakatos, *The methodology of scientific research programmes (Cambridge University Press, 1978).*

## NURTURING A WISE MIND

My grandson James was eight years old when he realized that he felt most comfortable with the LGBTQ+ community. He was eager to learn as much as he could, hoping to find his place in it. James was lucky; his mom encouraged him to express his true self, regardless of how other people might view him. He goes about life dancing like no one is watching, whether it's wearing expressive clothing or literally dancing in the chip aisle at a grocery store. He is embracing his personal discovery journey and becoming comfortable in his own skin.

James's bigger challenge, now that he is thirteen, is learning how to navigate being around people he doesn't like. He quickly becomes overstimulated and is working hard to develop coping skills. How wonderful that at such a young age, James understands the cards he was dealt and is intentionally developing strategies to win in life.

## UNTANGLE AND TAKE CHARGE

Teenage years are often referred to as "the difficult years," but I posit they are more simplistic and linear compared to the complexities of adulthood. Young adults quickly become enmeshed in supposed-tos, cultural constraints, restrictive taboos, and relationships. It takes intentional effort to untangle the cords that bind and hold us back. A strategy to help us pause and reflect when emotionally charged events occur makes a significant difference. Learning to self-regulate our emotions makes it possible to attain a feeling of peace.

My mindfulness mentor, Sylvia Boorstein, author, psychotherapist, and Buddhist teacher, encourages me to say to myself, *You are in pain, sweetheart* whenever I'm frustrated and feeling out of sorts. She encourages me to take a breath, pause, and remember that this moment will pass. It is not the end of all ends. My pain and frustration will ease, and life will go on.

One night, an Uber driver dropped Bill and me at a Day's Inn and drove away before we discovered that although our room was accessible, it was a long block away. A sign in front of the receptionist said that assistance for handicapped people would be happily provided when requested. When I asked for that assistance, the clerk looked at me blankly.

"I don't know of any sign. If you wanted wheelchair assistance, you should have written and requested it." (As if I knew ahead of time that accessible rooms would be a block away.)

I looked at the clerk, thinking about the pain and difficulty Bill would experience walking that far. Before I launched into a slice-and-dice job, I heard Sylvia whisper to me: "Imagine his life. A night clerk at an old motor motel who is paid minimum wage, lives in a modest dwelling, probably has an annoying roommate who plays video games all day and leaves dirty dishes strewn around. He's doing the best he can with the cards he was dealt. Send him a hearty dose of loving kindness instead of venting your frustration on him."

I followed Sylvia's advice and sprayed him with loving kindness, relieved to feel proud of myself versus wallowing in guilt, the likely aftermath of dumping my frustration on a powerless clerk. Thank you, Sylvia.

Researchers call this the "wisdom state of mind"—a flexible, caring, and composed disposition that enables us to fully leverage our cognitive abilities and meet situational demands. Quite frankly, I attribute my reaction in this case to timing. I was returning from a mindfulness retreat, and Sylvia's teachings were prominent in my mind. Lucky night clerk and lucky me.

## MISLEADING MYTHS

No matter where and how we grow up, whatever the environment, we all encounter societal myths that need not define us or our lives.

1. *Negative emotions are "bad" or "wrong."*

Give yourself permission to feel. As Sylvia says, "Pause. Acknowledge that you feel pain. Comfort yourself. Take a breath and remember that life will go on and this moment will soon pass."

2. *Another person can "make" you feel an emotion.*

People, places, smells, words, or colors, and factors like stress, conflict, criticism, failure, rejection, uncertainty, and a lack of control can trigger emotions. Our response to these triggers is the variable we can control. Experts suggest acknowledging and validating emotions rather than suppressing or ignoring them. Recommended strategies include practicing mindfulness, deep-breathing exercises, journaling, seeking social support, engaging in physical activity, and walking in nature. Explore it all, and once you identify the coping mechanisms that work for you, practice them consistently.

3. *Freedom of expression permits you to react explosively, no matter who you affect or hurt.*

Inciting violence, harassment, or defamation, spreading false information, cyberbullying, and speech that promotes discrimination or intolerance based on race, gender, religion, or sexual orientation is *never* okay. If that is the way you feel, acknowledge it, and then try to understand why. These forms of expression can cause harm, perpetuate stereotypes, and create divisions within communities. Focus instead on peaceful protest, artistic expression, constructive criticism, and social media engagement that promotes dialogue and understanding.

4. *Emotions get in the way of good decision-making.*

Not true! Emotions provide valuable insight and guidance. They can contribute to a holistic decision-making process that considers rational analysis and emotional intelligence.

Intuition often provides quick insight or gut feelings that can lead to rapid decision-making, particularly in situations where time is limited or information is incomplete. It is based on subconscious processing of a wealth of implicit knowledge and past experiences, so following your intuition can guide you toward choices that feel right on a deep level, aligned with your core values, beliefs, and aspirations. Intuition is often associated with creativity and innovation, as it can lead to unconventional ideas or solutions that may not be immediately obvious through rational analysis. Trusting intuition can boost your self-confidence and self-trust, empowering you to make bold decisions and take risks with conviction.

The idea that individuals can make successful decisions without deliberate analytical thought has intrigued philosophers and scientists since the ancient Greeks. Recently, a team of psychological scientists from the University of New South Wales devised a novel technique to demonstrate how much unconscious intuition can inform and even improve decision-making. The research team of Galang Lufityanto, Chris Donkin, and Joel Pearson published their findings in *Psychological Science*.[48] One fascinating discovery is that intuition improves over time. Getting out of your own head can lead to more intuitive thinking. Great leaders make smart decisions, even in difficult circumstances. From Albert Einstein to Oprah Winfrey, many top leaders ascribe their success to having followed their intuition.

*Empathy* helps you consider the impact of your decisions on those around you, leading to more compassionate and ethical choices.

*Curiosity* can help you find solutions that are not obvious and straightforward. Combined with creativity, you can develop ideas and intuitively know if something works or not.

*Optimism* and *gratitude* help you approach decision-making with confidence and resilience, even in the face of challenges or setbacks. By considering the positive aspects of different options, it is easier to

---

[48] Galang Lufityanto, Chris Donkin, and Joel Pearson, "Measuring Intuition: Nonconscious Emotional Information Boosts Decision Accuracy and Confidence," *Psychological Science*, 2016 May; 27(5):622–34.

appreciate the people you interact with and the opportunities you are privileged to experience.

5.  *You're too emotional, and that's bad.*

Hogwash! Be your own advocate. Act on what you intuit. Listen to your gut. Every time you accept and reflect on your experiences and emotions with curiosity and openness, you grow in self-love and gain inner peace.

Embrace uncertainty. Life is filled with ambiguity and uncontrollable events. By trusting yourself to deal with whatever happens, unlimited opportunities for learning and growth await.

Laugh. Find daily delights. We've had a hot summer, and the local critters gravitate to our water feature on the back patio. It's about three feet tall, a stacked multibowl "mini waterfall" affair. We chuckle when Tailor, the neighborhood squirrel, bushy tail straight in the air, attempts to drink, teetering on the rim of the bottom bowl. The most mundane things can bring joy.

## INTEGRITY AND ALIGNMENT

I want my actions to align with my values and principles—to act with honesty, authenticity, and compassion in all areas of my life. I'm not always successful, but I try.

Our lovely house cleaner, Rita, is a single mom who juggles many balls with few resources. She often texts me at the last minute that she can't show up as scheduled. After missing three consecutive weeks, we decided to find someone else. Bill wanted to relieve me of extra work, and I wanted to please Bill. Instead of telling Bill that I really didn't care if the house was dirty, I let Rita go. By the next week, overwhelmed with feelings of guilt for not supporting Rita during her struggles, I confessed my feelings to Bill, who promptly supported my desire to rehire her. Fortunately, Rita quickly agreed to return.

I know I am honorable and mean well, but I make mistakes, and I'm not always nice. I like to categorize these less desirable episodes as my "mountain on wheels" and roll them to the side while concentrating on my good stuff.

My friend Sara is a master of congruence and alignment. She strives to provide a haven for others by curating a retreat center (Rancho la Puerta) that embodies tranquility in Tecate, Mexico. Sara radiates peace, and the landscape demonstrates harmony between natural beauty—love for the land, for the people, plants, and animals inhabiting the land, and love for each other—and the human need for stimulating new ideas and exercise.

Shahram Heshmat, PhD, writes in "10 Sources of Wisdom" that a wise person is not primarily guided by her immediate actions but by the ultimate goals of her *entire* life.[49] A broader perspective makes it easier to put complicating details aside and focus on what seems most important. Having a sense of direction or purpose is associated with emotional stability and resilience during vulnerable and stressful life events.

## ACCESSING OUR POWER

"Mindfulness" and "meditation" are terms often used interchangeably, but there is a basic difference.

Mindfulness improves self-awareness by encouraging us to notice what is happening in the present moment without interpretation or judgment. It is a practice we can experience wherever we go by noticing what we are seeing, feeling, smelling, and touching. By focusing on the present moment and tuning out everything else, we can listen to ourselves, strengthen our ability to regulate our emotions, and become more compassionate, especially with ourselves. Mindfulness can serve

---

49   Shahram Heshmat, PhD, "10 Sources of Wisdom," *Psychology Today*, October 19, 2023, https://www.psychologytoday.com/us/blog/science-of-choice/202101/10-sources-of-wisdom.

as a body-and-mind scan, taking our temperature on what we are feeling. Silence and stillness allow our intuition to breathe so we can hear our inner voices. This frees us up to become less impulsive and make wiser decisions.

Meditation is an exercise that helps us focus our thoughts and discipline our bodies. It organizes the mind to prevent mental clutter so we can pay attention to our inner selves. There's mantra meditation, guided meditation, and transcendental meditation. We can meditate alone or with a meditation teacher in group settings or classes.

When I am trying to fall asleep, the repetitiveness of mantra meditation—repeating the same phrases over and over—corrals the random thoughts in my head. It soothes me by modulating my emotions and focusing my self-talk. Success is when I *remember* to recite my mantra when annoyed by difficult situations or feel myself becoming impatient. I want my inner mind to only have space for thoughts of peace, love, and harmony, but it won't happen unless I make time and practice.

## A Global Visionary

In 1941, Vijali Hamilton was an orphan being raised by nuns. One day, she sat in the dirt and drew a circle around her tiny two-year-old body. Vijali believes that she intuitively understood her calling: to travel around the earth and help Indigenous people reconnect with their land and find peace. She allowed her intuition to guide her and the energy of her empathy and compassion to fuel her growth. Vijali recognized her purpose. Her next step was to gain the skills to accomplish it.

In her midforties, Vijali started on her first "world wheel," a seven-year spiritual and artistic pilgrimage, armed with a bag of sculpting tools and her camera. She circled the globe on the thirty-fourth latitudinal parallel, creating monumental stone sculptures and community-based ceremony performances in twelve countries, including in the Middle East, India, Tibet, China, Siberia, and Japan.

By the time Vijali began the second world wheel, Global Peace through the Arts, in 1999, she was a recognized sculptor, filmmaker, poet, musician, and author with more than a thousand artworks placed in museums, public spaces, and private collections. During her second sojourn around the planet, Vijali collaborated with diversified communities in the Andes and the Amazon of Ecuador, as well as Africa, Australia, and the Republic of Georgia.

Vijali's latest books—*World Wheel: One Woman's Quest for Peace, Of Earth and Fire* (poetry and art) and *Liberty: Enlightening the World* (poetry and art), as well as her feature film, *Wheel of the World: One Woman's Creative Journey for Global Peace*—are available through Amazon and her website, worldwheel.org.

## WELCOME TO THE WISE WOMEN SISTERHOOD

Wisdom is a process that requires us to be a student and a teacher. As we strive to reach our fullest potential, here are some vital mindsets to guide our path forward:

- ✦ I am *curious* and *open-minded*. I want to learn, explore new ideas, understand different perspectives, and savor new experiences.
- ✦ I am *empathetic* and *compassionate*. I want to support and comfort those in need of emotional and spiritual healing.
- ✦ I will *teach* and *share what I have learned*. I will withstand scrutiny and criticism and leverage my experience with courage.
- ✦ I desire to *foster deep, nurturing connections*. I will strive to bring

people together, facilitate collaboration, and create networks that support mutual growth and development.
- I *relieve myself of the burden of always being right.* I do not know all the answers. It is okay to make mistakes. I forgive myself for not being perfect.
- I strive to *balance "being" with "doing."* I will practice self-care by making time and allowing space for me, recognizing I have limited energy and a need to recharge.
- I *know who I am.* I have discovered my authentic self. I am the one who has chosen the values that control my moral compass.
- I am *aligned.* My mind, body, and spirit strive to follow the same path.
- I *possess a deep reservoir of wisdom, insight, and understanding.* I will let my light shine and allow my sisters to light their candles in my flame.

# DREAM:
## *Recognizing My Wise Woman Within*

**D**esire: Continue to evolve, trusting my intuition to help me reach my full potential.

**R**eflect on my knowledge and experiences to gain insights.

**E**xplore the ways in which I may light the paths of others to ease their journeys.

**A**knowledge that I have wisdom worthy of sharing.

**M**antra:
Let me be open-minded and learn from others.
Let me connect and bring people together.
Let me comfort and promote spiritual well-being.
Let me protect and preserve what is valuable and meaningful.
Let me approach challenges with innovation, adaptability, and imagination.
Let me explore the unknown with curiosity and courage.
Let me share what I learn and empower those around me.

## WISE WOMAN WORDS

"Wisdom has been around since eternity and will be there forever more. It is our responsibility to recognize the light that is within us, every one of us. Each of us has the possibility, the probability, the potential, to be the light on somebody else's path."
—*Maya Angelou*

# Epilogue

**M**y "DREAM" *is to be an erga and make the path to serenity easier for others.*

**D**esire: By sharing my story and reflections, more women will begin to access and share their wisdom, and the world will become more compassionate, and life fairer.

**R**eflect on ways to encourage women of all ages and interest groups, societies, and cultures to seek knowledge with open minds and to carve out time to reflect and assimilate their learning.

**E**xplore the technology, platforms, messaging, and venues that will provide the broadest reach.

**A**cknowledge that we need to motivate leaders of all ages, skills, ethnicities, religions, societies, and cultures to step forward and collaborate.

**M**antra:
Guide and protect us as we . . .
Seek knowledge with open minds.
Reflect on learning without bias.
Speak clearly and persuasively.
Give us strength to promote
Peace and understanding
In this fractured and hurting world.

# Acknowledgments

I am where I am, doing what I do, because of the millions of people who have touched my life. I am a composite being, made up of bits and pieces of flotsam and stardust, too many to count and too scattered to define. Plainly put . . . I'm just damn lucky. I have been at the right place at the right time and have reaped benefits from incredible opportunities. Humbled and honored, I thank you, guides.

The title, *The Magic of Yes*, became fixated in my mind the second I saw that little girl with flies on her face in the Sahara Desert. I felt myself physically stepping beyond fear, embarking on a magical journey into the unknown. I had no idea where I was going or what I was going to do; I just knew that except for fate, that little girl with flies in her eyes could have been my darling granddaughter Ella. I had no choice. I had to act. All little girls and boys deserve the chance to have a healthy life.

The eight years I lived in Ethiopia were thrilling, exhausting, frustrating, and satisfying. In October 2016, when forced to leave the country, my energy level was zero. I had nothing more to give. It took over six years of Bill's nurturing and the healing power of love to replenish me.

I knew without question that writing *The Magic of Yes* was the one supposed-to I had to do. Compelled to share what I learned, with a hundred pages of notes in hand, I searched for someone to help me. Once again, my guides took charge and steered me to my editor, David Tabatsky. He structured the lessons I've learned and insights I've gained into this guidebook and gave me the confidence to write my own story. Hannah Woodlan, Koehler Books, has done a magnificent job of making my story and bits of wisdom sing to the magical score designed by Danielle and her team. Kathleen Schmidt, publicist extraordinaire, has engineered my path as an author and reluctant user of social media.

Lady Luck (my guides) continues to feed me by folding old friends and new acquaintances into my journey at exactly the right time. My kids, Melissa, Shay, and David, encourage me; my grandkids are my cheerleaders; my dear friend Megan Tarnow is my erga, making it easier for me to grapple with today's technology. And to all my early readers who slogged through draft chapters and gave me insightful feedback, thank you, thank you. I appreciate each of you and am so thankful you are in my life.

I want to give special thanks to the extraordinary ordinary women who allowed me to include snippets of their amazing journeys in *The Magic of Yes*. Daily, more extraordinary ordinary women volunteer to share their stories in my newsletter, *Sticky Thoughts*. The courage, bravery, and willingness shown by these women humble me. Thank you for allowing me into your lives.

And to my heart's delight, Bill Butcher, my insightful sounding board, constant supporter, and bravest critic. Thank you for being the best partner a girl could ever have—and for loving and accepting me so completely.

www.ingramcontent.com/pod-product-compliance
Lightning Source LLC
LaVergne TN
LVHW091541070526
838199LV00002B/161